The Secret to
TESLA'S
Stock Market Success

Daluxe Inc.

The Secret to Tesla's Stock Market Success

Copyright Page

© 2024 by Daluxe Inc. All rights reserved.

No part of this book may be reproduced, stored in a retrieval system, or transmitted in any form or by any means, electronic, mechanical, photocopying, recording, scanning, or otherwise, except as permitted under the Canadian *Copyright Act*, R.S.C., 1985, c. C-42, without prior written permission from the publisher.

This book is protected under Canadian copyright laws. Any reproduction or unauthorized use of the material or artwork contained herein is prohibited without the express written consent of the publisher.

This book is intended solely for informational and educational purposes. It should not be used as a substitute for professional, financial, or legal advice. The author and publisher make no representations or warranties, express or implied, regarding the completeness, accuracy, reliability, or suitability of the information provided in the book. Any reliance placed on such information is strictly at your own risk.

Please consult with a professional advisor or attorney before making any financial decisions based on the content of this book. The author and publisher are not responsible for errors, inaccuracies, or omissions. They shall not be liable for any loss or damage, including, but not limited to, any direct, indirect, incidental, consequential, or special damages arising from or in connection with the use of this book or its information.

Daluxe Inc.

The Secret to Tesla's Stock Market Success

Table of Contents

Introduction 9
    Welcome to the Journey 9
    Why Tesla? 9
Chapter 1: The Rise of Tesla in the Age of Disruption 11
    The Fourth Industrial Revolution: What Is It? 12
    The Electric Vehicle Revolution: More Than Just a Trend 13
    Tesla's Role in the Future 14
    Powering the Future: Tesla and Renewable Energy 15
    Optimus: Tesla's Humanoid Revolution 15
    Disruption: Tesla's Recipe for Market Mayhem 16
    Why Tesla's Trajectory Matters for Investors 17
Chapter 2: A Brief History of Tesla 19
    Founding and Early Years 19
    Elon Musk's Vision 21
    Elon Musk's Compensation Package 24
    Growth and Expansion 27
Chapter 3: The Influence of Seasons on Tesla's Stock Performance .. 31
    The Spring Surge 32
    Summer Stability 37
    Autumn Adjustments 41

Daluxe Inc.

Winter Woes and Wins 45

Chapter 4: Analyzing Tesla's Financial Health 51

    Quarterly Reports Overview 51

    Key Metrics to Watch 54

Chapter 5: The Role of Innovation 59

    Tesla's Technological Advancements 59

    Impact of New Releases 64

Chapter 6: External Influences 69

    Economic Factors 69

Chapter 7: Case Studies 81

    How to Get Tesla's Quarterly Report and How to Analyze It ... 81

    Case Study: The Comprehensive Investor – Sarah's Journey ... 84

    Internal Factors 84

    External Factors: Economic and Regulatory Environment 101

    Seasonal Factors 111

    The Decision: A Well-Informed Investment 111

Chapter 8: The Role of Stagflation in Tesla's Stock Movements ... 125

    Analyzing Economic Signals and Tesla's Stock Performance ... 126

    What is a Recession? An Explanation of Economic Downturns .. 129

    How to Predict a Recession Using Economic Indicators 130

    Recession vs. Stagflation: Economic Downturn vs. High Inflation and Unemployment 133

    The Impact of Stagflation on Tesla's Stock Performance 134

Chapter 9: Algo Trading and Tesla Stock: Understanding High-Frequency Movements 139

Predictive Models and Tools 139

Time Series Analysis 140

Example of Time Series Analysis on Tesla Stock 140

Machine Learning 147

Machine Learning and Timing Tesla's Stock 149

Chapter 10: The Future of Tesla Stock: Beyond Cars 155

Tesla Energy: Powering More Than Cars 155

Tesla as an AI-Driven Tech Company 159

RoboTaxi and Tesla's Growth: The Self-Driving Revolution 162

Optimus Robot: From Manufacturing to Healthcare 164

Robotaxi: A Game-Changer for Revenue 167

Reference List 170

Daluxe Inc.

Introduction

Welcome to the Journey

Welcome, dear reader, to a thrilling expedition through the electrifying world through the wild, ever-shifting world of Tesla stock! This book is not your typical dry stock market manual—it's a blend of academic insight and friendly conversation, peppered with just enough humor to keep you from dozing off between pages. Think of it as your personal guide to cracking the code of Tesla's market movements while enjoying the ride.

Why Tesla?

Why focus on Tesla amidst the vast sea of stocks? Tesla is not just a car manufacturer; it's a revolutionary force reshaping the automotive, artificial intelligence, and electric energy sectors. Founded by the enigmatic Elon Musk, Tesla has become synonymous with innovation, sustainability, and, let's face it, a bit of stock market drama. And you, dear reader, hold a unique position.

Daluxe Inc.

You have the privilege to delve into the depths of its stock cycles, a journey that promises to be as enlightening as exciting.

We'll explore the economic forces, government policies, and tech innovations that make Tesla the stock to watch. From the rise of AI and autonomous driving to the disruption of global supply chains, this book will equip you with the tools to navigate Tesla's peaks, dips, and every twist in between.

Chapter 1: The Rise of Tesla in the Age of Disruption

Did you know that the Tesla Model 3 has a quirky feature called "Emissions Testing Mode" - which is a fart mode? Yes, you heard that right. You can prank your passengers by making the car emit fart sounds from any seat in the vehicle. And, of course, you can control it with the steering wheel buttons. Although not directly connected to the car's performance, this creative and fun feature adds to Tesla's brand image and customer loyalty. Tesla is changing both transportation and comedy and influencing its stock performance!

Daluxe Inc.

Let's transition from flatulent noises to something equally revolutionary - Tesla's role in the Fourth Industrial Revolution. We're delving into how Tesla is more than just a car company; it's molding the future of AI, automation, and clean energy. Whether you're a technology enthusiast, an investor, or simply curious, you'll want to watch Tesla's impact on the world.

The Fourth Industrial Revolution: What Is It?

The First Industrial Revolution started in the late 1700s, marked by the creation of steam engines, railroads, and factories. This period brought about a significant shift from agrarian lifestyles to factory work involving the operation of large machinery.

Moving ahead to the late 1800s, the Second Industrial Revolution emerged as the era of electricity, mass production, and assembly lines. The world became a place where we could quickly make A LOT of stuff.

By the mid-1900s, the Third Industrial Revolution - the Digital Revolution - arrived. Today, we have computers, the internet, and all the interconnectedness that defines today's world. That's why your fridge can now talk to your smartphone (not that they have anything interesting to say).

The Secret to Tesla's Stock Market Success

We're entering the Fourth Industrial Revolution, a period where our physical, digital, and biological worlds are merging. This revolution is characterized by the rapid advancement of technologies such as artificial intelligence, robotics, quantum computing, 3D printing, and biotechnology. Tesla is leading the way with its innovations in these areas, and, to everyone's surprise, it is at the heart of all this excitement.

The Electric Vehicle Revolution: More Than Just a Trend

In the past, electric vehicles (EVs) were often perceived less favorably. They were small, unattractive cars with a limited range, hardly capable of traveling across town without requiring a recharge. However, Tesla revolutionized the perception of EVs, transforming them into symbols of sophistication, speed, and desirability. The Roadster, in particular, exemplified a remarkable fusion of power and elegance. At the same time, the Model S redefined the driving experience by integrating electric propulsion with environmental mindfulness, futuristic design, and luxury.

Tesla didn't just stop at making great cars; they've redefined what transportation could be. When you're behind the wheel of a Tesla, it's not just about getting from point A to point B—it's about doing it with style, efficiency, and a sprinkle of cutting-edge tech. As the world began to shift toward greener solutions, Tesla became a beacon of the future of mobility.

Tesla's Role in the Future

While most people consider Tesla an electric car company, it's much more. Tesla is deeply involved in AI, self-driving technology, and renewable energy solutions. Their self-driving cars are not just cool gadgets - they're powered by AI that can navigate roads, avoid obstacles, and transport passengers safely - all without a human driver. This is not just a revolution; it's a leap into the future.

Tesla's roboTaxi envisions a fleet of fully autonomous vehicles. Users can summon a car via an app, relax as it drives, and even earn money while it gives rides to others. This innovation offers a new way of transportation, replacing traditional ride-hailing services like Uber.

Who is responsible if a Tesla roboTaxi crashes? If a human driver causes an accident, they are held accountable, but in the case of a roboTaxi, it's a gray area. Some believe that the car manufacturer (Tesla) could be liable for faulty software or hardware accidents. At the same time, Tesla might argue that users accept the risks when summoning the car.

Tesla has recently launched its own insurance service, signaling a potential shift in how insurance claims will be managed for autonomous vehicles. It's evident that Tesla is causing significant disruptions in the automotive industry, insurance sector, and overall transportation landscape.

Powering the Future: Tesla and Renewable Energy

Tesla isn't just electrifying cars; it's electrifying the world. Their solar panels and Powerwall batteries bring clean energy to homes and businesses. Imagine harnessing the sun's energy, storing it in your Powerwall, and using it to charge your Tesla. No grid? No problem. The Powerwall is designed to keep your home powered even when the grid fails.

This isn't just about convenience - it's a glimpse into a future where we're less reliant on fossil fuels and more integrated with sustainable energy.

Optimus: Tesla's Humanoid Revolution

Tesla's latest creation, Optimus, is an AI-powered humanoid robot capable of lifting 45 pounds. It is designed to revolutionize various industries by performing factory tasks, providing support in hazardous environments, and assisting older people with daily activities. Thanks to its advanced AI systems, Optimus is elegant, versatile, and safe around humans. Tesla's move into robotics with Optimus demonstrates the company's dedication to innovation and problem-solving. Whether it's assembling cars at Gigafactories or serving as a future companion for those in need, Optimus signals a new era in robotics, showcasing Tesla's ever-expanding potential.

Disruption: Tesla's Recipe for Market Mayhem

Tesla isn't just a stock you buy because everyone else is buying it (though sometimes it feels that way when the price jumps after Elon tweets). It's a stock representing a shift in how we think about the future—whether in mobility, energy, or even artificial intelligence. The company's long-term trajectory is rooted in its ability to disrupt multiple industries simultaneously, making it a unique opportunity for investors willing to see the bigger picture.

Tesla has significantly influenced various industries by introducing innovative and disruptive technologies, effectively reshaping markets with a strong emphasis on innovation. The company's primary objective is to redefine entire industries rather than solely offering superior products.

What makes Tesla particularly exciting is that the auto industry's limits do not confine it. When you invest in Tesla, you're not just investing in a car company. You're investing in the future of renewable energy, AI-driven technologies, and robotics. It's a journey that promises to be as thrilling as it is profitable.

Tesla's impact extends beyond the automotive sector, challenging the traditional reliance on gasoline and exerting influence on the stock prices of competing automakers, as well as the long-term viability of oil and gas investments. Understanding Tesla's industry disruption is imperative for investors, as investing in Tesla represents more than a stake in a car company – it symbolizes a commitment to a new technological, transportation, and energy paradigm.

Why Tesla's Trajectory Matters for Investors

Tesla is, after all, one of the most talked-about and debated stocks on Wall Street. Its price can swing wildly based on everything from quarterly earnings to Elon's musings on social media. For savvy investors, this volatility isn't something to fear—it's something to harness. It's an opportunity to make strategic moves and capitalize on the market's fluctuations.

In the Age of Disruption, Tesla represents the promise of tomorrow and the wild unpredictability of breaking away from the past. The question isn't whether Tesla will keep disrupting industries—it's how prepared you are to time your investments as it does.

So, buckle up. We're just getting started. The future promises to be as exhilarating as unpredictable, and Tesla is at the forefront of this thrilling journey.

Chapter 2: A Brief History of Tesla

Founding and Early Years

The founding of Tesla is a tale that reads like a Silicon Valley fairytale, complete with visionaries, bold ideas, and a sprinkle of controversy. In 2003, two brave engineers, Martin Eberhard and Marc Tarpenning, decided to take on the automotive giants with nothing more than a dream and a garage. They faced numerous challenges, from securing funding in a skeptical market to convincing the public about the viability of electric cars. But they were undeterred. Yes, every excellent startup story begins in a garage. It's practically a rule.

Far from being typical gearheads, Eberhard and Tarpenning were driven by an audacious vision of a cleaner, greener future powered by electricity. They dared to dream of building electric cars that were not just eco-friendly but also sleek, fast, and desirable. Their commitment to innovation was unparalleled. Thus, Tesla Motors was born and named after the legendary inventor Nikola Tesla, who knew something about electric power himself. Their audacity to dream big and challenge the status quo is truly inspiring.

Elon Musk, the entrepreneur who would come to embody Tesla, joined Tesla in 2004, spearheading the company's initial investment round and assuming the role of chairman. His strategic choices and unwavering faith in the impossible were pivotal in shaping Tesla's early years. Think of Musk as the fairy godfather, but instead of a magic wand, he brandished a substantial checkbook and an unshakable belief in the impossible. His involvement gave Tesla the financial strength and audacious vision to realize its lofty aspirations.

The early years of Tesla were anything but smooth sailing. But Tesla's founders were undeterred. They created a car to blow the competition out of the water. The road to success was littered with obstacles, from production delays to cost overruns and a near-death experience during the 2008 financial crisis. Yet, through it all, Tesla's team demonstrated a remarkable tenacity, a testament to their unwavering dedication and perhaps a hint of madness, fueling their relentless pursuit of their vision.

The Secret to Tesla's Stock Market Success

The early years of Tesla stand as a testament to the power of visionary thinking and relentless perseverance. From its humble beginnings in a modest garage to the unveiling of the Roadster, Tesla's journey was a rollercoaster of challenges and triumphs.

Elon Musk's Vision

Regarding visionary leaders, Elon Musk is in a league of his own. Think of him as a modern-day Da Vinci with more rockets and less painting. Musk's vision for Tesla isn't just about building electric cars but transforming the entire transportation and energy landscape. For instance, Tesla's Gigafactory has revolutionized battery production, making electric vehicles more accessible and affordable. Let's dive into the mind of the man who wants to change the world one Tesla at a time.

A World of Sustainable Energy

Imagine a world where your car doesn't guzzle gas like a marathon runner at a water station. Instead, it sips electricity produced by the sun. This car is the cornerstone of Musk's vision: to transition the world to sustainable energy. Tesla isn't just about electric vehicles but an integrated renewable energy system. For instance, Tesla's Powerwalls are home batteries that store energy for a rainy day, ensuring a continuous supply of clean energy. Solar roofs power your home, and sleek electric vehicles make gas guzzlers look like dinosaurs. Musk's dream is to make this clean energy ecosystem the norm rather than the exception.

Innovation Beyond Cars

Musk's ambitions don't stop at your driveway. He envisions a world where Tesla's innovations permeate every aspect of our energy consumption. Picture solar panels as standard as lawn gnomes and home batteries that make power outages a thing of the past. The 'Tesla Ecosystem' is designed to allow you to generate, store, and use renewable energy seamlessly. It's like having a personal, eco-friendly power plant in your backyard.

Autonomous Driving

If you think self-driving cars are something out of a sci-fi movie, think again. Musk is turning that fiction into reality. Tesla's Autopilot and Full Self-Driving (FSD) technologies are leading the charge toward a future where you can nap during your commute. These technologies use advanced sensors and AI to navigate city streets and highways without a human touching the wheel.

The Secret to Tesla's Stock Market Success

Mass-Market Affordability

Musk's strategy is not just about catering to the elite; it's about ensuring everyone can afford a Tesla. Introducing the Model 3 was a game-changer, bringing the luxury of electric vehicles to the masses. Musk's brilliant strategy is to use the profits from high-end models like the Model S and Model X to subsidize the development of more affordable cars. Tesla is not just about making great cars; it's about ensuring everyone can be a part of a sustainable future.

Innovative Manufacturing

What's a visionary plan without a revolutionary way to execute it? The Gigafactory isn't just a factory; it's a colossal cathedral of innovation dedicated to producing batteries and vehicles at an unprecedented scale. By manufacturing batteries in-house, Tesla reduces costs and improves efficiency. Musk's approach to vertical integration ensures that Tesla can meet growing demand while maintaining quality. It's like Willy Wonka's factory but for electric cars instead.

A Bold Future

Musk's vision is nothing if not audacious. He's not content with making great cars; he wants to redefine the future of energy and transportation. His relentless pursuit of innovation has positioned Tesla as a leader in both industries. Musk's forward-thinking approach tackles global challenges head-on, from climate change to energy sustainability. It's not just about Tesla's success; it's about creating a better, cleaner world for everyone.

In conclusion, Elon Musk's vision for Tesla is much more than cars. It's about creating a sustainable, innovative future where clean energy is accessible. So, next time you see a Tesla, remember: you're not just looking at a car; you're looking at a piece of the future, handcrafted by a modern visionary.

Elon Musk's Compensation Package

Regarding compensation packages, most CEOs might settle for an excellent salary, a hefty bonus, and a smattering of stock options. However, Elon Musk, being Elon Musk, decided to throw the corporate playbook out the window and rewrite it in a language only he truly understands. His compensation plan is a stark departure from industry norms, which typically include a mix of salary, bonuses, and stock options. Instead, Musk's plan is entirely tied to Tesla's performance, a structure that makes typical corporate pay look like pocket change. Strap in because Musk's compensation package is a story of audacious ambition, jaw-dropping figures, and a structure that is truly unique in the corporate world.

The Secret to Tesla's Stock Market Success

In 2018, Tesla's board of directors unveiled a compensation plan for Musk that can only be described as a daring leap of faith. There was no salary, no cash bonuses, and Musk's compensation was entirely tied to the company's performance. If Tesla thrived, Musk would thrive; if Tesla floundered, Musk would earn zilch. This compensation plan was not just a financial strategy but a bold statement of Musk's unwavering commitment to Tesla's success, a commitment that he was willing to back with his entire compensation.

The package was structured around milestones that were considered progressively challenging video game levels. Each milestone corresponded to a significant increase in Tesla's market value and operational performance targets. For instance, the first milestone required Tesla to reach a market capitalization of $100 billion, the second $200 billion, and so on. For every milestone Musk hit, he would unlock a new tranche of stock options, each worth a king's ransom.

These milestones required Tesla to grow from a market capitalization of $50 billion to a staggering $650 billion. Yes, you read that right—650 billion dollars. Musk needed to guide Tesla to achieve this astronomical growth within ten years. The milestones were not just lofty; they were stratospheric, designed to push both Musk and Tesla to the outer limits of possibility.

Each stock option that Musk unlocked allowed him to purchase shares at a significantly reduced price. If he achieved all the milestones, the total value of his stock options would be in the tens of billions of dollars. This plan not only aligned Musk's interests with Musk's shareholders but Tesla's also served as a powerful reassurance of his unwavering commitment to the company. If the company soared, so would Musk's compensation; if it didn't, he'd have to scrape by with his other ventures like SpaceX, Starlink, and The Boring Company.

Now, why such a complex and exquisite compensation plan? The answer lies in Musk's approach to leadership and vision. Musk demonstrated his unwavering commitment to the company's long-term goals by tying his financial rewards directly to Tesla's. This approach incentivized short-term performance and encouraged long-term strategic thinking and innovation. It's betting your entire fortune on a single hand of poker. This unique approach to compensation has shaped Tesla's future direction and its ability to innovate in the highly competitive automotive and energy sectors.

The audacity of Musk's compensation package caused quite a stir in the business world. Some hailed it as a brilliant move that incentivized extraordinary performance. Others saw it as a high-stakes gamble with shareholder money. Its impact on shareholder perception and trust was a key concern. While some shareholders were reassured by Musk's alignment of his interests with those of the company, others were worried about the potential for the plan to be misaligned with long-term shareholder value. Musk's go-big-or-go-home philosophy has long shaped Tesla's future and its relationship with its shareholders.

Musk's compensation package is more than just a pay plan. It's a statement of his confidence in Tesla and his relentless drive to push boundaries. So, the next time you hear about Tesla's market cap hitting new highs, remember that Elon Musk is probably grinning somewhere, knowing that he's a step closer to unlocking another level in his epic compensation game.

Growth and Expansion

Suppose Tesla's founding and early years were like the first cautious steps of a toddler. In that case, its growth and expansion phase resembles that same toddler discovering a candy stash and zooming around with uncontainable energy. From its modest beginnings, Tesla has become a powerhouse redefining industries and making headlines with its relentless pace of innovation and ambition.

After the Tesla Roadster proved that electric cars could be fast and sexy, Tesla set its sights on bigger, bolder horizons. The next milestone on this electrifying journey was the Model S, unveiled in 2012. The Model S wasn't just a car; it was a statement. Here was a luxury sedan that could outpace sports cars, run over 300 miles on a single charge, and still have room for groceries. It was the automotive equivalent of finding out your mild-mannered accountant moonlights as a superhero.

With the Model S, Tesla didn't just compete with other electric vehicles; it aimed squarely at the heart of the luxury car market, taking on titans like BMW and Mercedes-Benz. And guess what? It didn't just succeed. It revolutionized the game. The Model S not only racked up awards and rave reviews but also set a new standard for the industry, paving the way for Tesla's meteoric rise.

But Musk and his merry band of innovators weren't content with just one hit. They introduced the Model X, Tesla's answer to the SUV craze, with features that were not just practical but also cool. Launched in 2015, the Model X featured falcon-wing doors that looked like something straight out of a sci-fi movie. It perfectly blended functionality and fun, proving that electric SUVs could be both.

The next step in Tesla's grand plan was to bring electric driving to the masses. The Model 3, released in 2017, was designed to be an affordable, mass-market electric car. It was Tesla's moonshot—a gamble that paid off spectacularly. The company faced significant production hiccups, which Musk called 'production hell.' Despite these obstacles, the Model 3 emerged

The Secret to Tesla's Stock Market Success

victorious, solidifying Tesla's place in the automotive hall of fame.

While Tesla was busy conquering the car market, it was also making waves in the energy sector. The acquisition of SolarCity in 2016 marked a bold move into solar energy, aligning with Musk's vision of a sustainable future. Tesla's solar products, like the Solar Roof and Powerwall, aimed to create a seamless, integrated approach to clean energy for homes and businesses.

The gigafactory, Tesla's massive battery production facility, was initially built in Nevada and later expanded to other locations worldwide. This facility was crucial in lowering battery costs and increasing production capacity. It was often compared to Willy Wonka's Chocolate Factory, but instead of candy, it produced high-tech batteries for powering Tesla's expanding range of vehicles.

As if dominating the car and energy markets wasn't enough, Tesla also ventured into autonomous driving technology. The development of Tesla's Autopilot and Full Self-Driving (FSD) capabilities turned heads and sparked debates. Could a Tesla drive itself? Well, sort of. Musk's vision of fully autonomous vehicles is still a work in progress, but Tesla's advanced driver-assistance systems have already set new standards for safety and innovation.

Daluxe Inc.

In a few years, Tesla transformed from a scrappy startup into a global juggernaut, leading the charge in electric vehicles and renewable energy. The company's growth and expansion have been spectacular, marked by bold decisions, innovative products, and the occasional chaos.

So, as we zoom through Tesla's growth and expansion phase, it's clear that the company's journey is far from over. With ambitious plans for new models, energy solutions, and autonomous technology, Tesla's future looks as bright as a fully charged battery on a sunny day.

Chapter 3: The Influence of Seasons on Tesla's Stock Performance

"Every phenomenon has its cycle" was the sentiment the 1960s musical group The Byrds expressed. Like the natural world's patterns, Tesla's stock experiences phases of advancement, regression, and unforeseen fluctuations. Understanding these cycles is like finding a secret map hidden in the jungle of market volatility. This chapter will explore the seasonal trends that influence Tesla's stock behavior.

Tesla's stock price doesn't just march to the beat of Wall Street; it dances along to the rhythms of its production, sales, and external market influences. Over the years, several distinct seasonal patterns have emerged, allowing those with keen eyes and steady nerves to make well-timed investment decisions.

The Spring Surge

Historical Spring Trends

In this analysis, we examined the historical spring trends for Tesla's stock, treating them like an annual performance review, full of surprises and excitement, much like waiting to see if the groundhog will see its shadow. Tesla's stock may exhibit a spring fever, shaking off the doldrums of the colder months. This seasonal uptick isn't just driven by the longer days, warmer temperatures, and a confluence of factors that make spring an exciting time for Tesla enthusiasts and investors alike.

The spring surge in Tesla's stock is thrilling, fueled by a potent mix of product launches, financial performance, consumer behavior, market optimism, and the ever-charismatic Elon Musk. Tesla's stock often follows suit, offering a season of growth and opportunity. So, don your sunglasses and embark on a dazzling springtime ride with Tesla.

The Secret to Tesla's Stock Market Success

Factors Driving the Spring Surge

Springtime for Tesla's stock is like watching a garden come to life after a long winter. Suddenly, everything's in bloom, and the air buzzes with excitement. But what exactly fuels this annual resurgence? Let's dive into the bouquet of factors that drive Tesla's stock skyward every spring.

Product Announcements and Releases

One pivotal driver of Tesla's springtime buzz is the company's penchant for product announcements and releases during this season. Whether it's a new vehicle model, software updates, or advancements in battery technology, these announcements reverberate through the market, propelling the stock upward.

Earnings Reports

Spring is also earnings season, and Tesla's quarterly earnings reports can be as exhilarating or nerve-wracking as a roller coaster ride. Investors eagerly await the release of these reports, dissecting every detail for signs of growth, profitability, and prospects. A positive earnings report can send Tesla's stock soaring like a bird taking flight after being cooped up all winter or vice versa.

Market Sentiment and Speculation

Let's remember the ever-present force of market sentiment and speculation. Market sentiment refers to investors' feelings and beliefs about the market and its future direction. As the days grow longer and the mood lightens, investors often become more optimistic, buoyed by the broader economic trends that tend to improve with the advent of spring. This collective optimism can fuel higher stock prices, creating a self-fulfilling growth prophecy.

Historical Performance Data

The historical data shows a pattern of upward movement in Tesla's stock during the spring months. For instance, March through May has seen significant gains in several past years, sometimes outperforming other times of the year. Understanding and leveraging this data can empower investors to make informed decisions.

The Musk Effect

Tesla's stock's spring trends are undoubtedly intricately tied to the profound Musk effect. With his charismatic leadership and bold announcements, Elon Musk often becomes the catalyst behind Tesla's springtime buzz. His influence on the stock resembles a coach who ignites the team's spirit just in time for the big game.

The Secret to Tesla's Stock Market Success

Investors' Strategies

Successful investors have observed and strategically anticipated these springtime trends, adjusting their strategies accordingly. However, it's important to note that these trends are not without risks. Despite these challenges, historical spring trends for Tesla's stock reveal a season of opportunity, growth, and excitement. Like the budding flowers and chirping birds, Tesla's stock often comes to life in the spring, buoyed by product launches, earnings reports, and Elon Musk's indefatigable enthusiasm.

Tax Season and Refund Spending

Tax season is when many people find a little extra cash thanks to their refunds. And what better way to spend that windfall than investing in a company as exciting as Tesla? This influx of disposable income often finds its way into the stock market, boosting demand for shares and pushing prices up. Think of it as a spring cleaning bonus that goes straight into your investment portfolio.

Seasonal Increase in Car Sales

Spring is also the prime car-buying season. Tesla's stylish, eco-friendly vehicles become particularly attractive. An uptick in car sales, especially for new models, boosts revenue and investor confidence. It's like swapping out your old, rusty bike for a shiny new Tesla—there's no comparison.

Innovation and Technological Advances

Tesla's relentless drive for innovation doesn't take a season off. Spring often brings news of cutting-edge developments in self-driving technology, energy solutions, and manufacturing processes. Each breakthrough reinforces Tesla's position as a market leader, driving investor enthusiasm and stock prices upward. For instance, Optimus, the Tesla Bot, is not just a walking automaton. It's a strategic move that symbolizes Tesla's ambitions to revolutionize industries beyond electric vehicles and space travel. Optimus holds the potential to impact Tesla's stock price significantly.

With new revenue streams, cost savings, technological leadership, and market disruption, Tesla could see its stock soar. This potential for financial gain should instill a sense of optimism and confidence in investors, making them feel like they've made a wise investment in the high-stakes game of stock market poker. It's like finding out your favorite band is releasing a new album—it's exciting and makes you want to invest even more.

The Secret to Tesla's Stock Market Success

Summer Stability

Summer Performance Patterns

It's the season of beach trips, barbecues, and a curious dance of stock stability and subtle shifts for Tesla investors. If the stock market were a high school, Summer would be an excellent teacher who lets everyone relax but keeps a watchful eye on things. Let's take a detailed look at Tesla's stock behavior during the summer months and see how it tends to perform when the sun is shining brightly.

Historically, Tesla's stock is stable during the summer months, with fewer dramatic spikes and drops compared to other seasons. This period can often feel like the calm in the eye of a financial hurricane, providing a sense of security to investors. One reason for this stability is the lack of major product launches or announcements, which typically occur in the spring or fall. Without the excitement of new products to stir the pot, the stock tends to hover around a steady range, basking in the summer sun.

In June, as the second quarter draws to a close, investors keenly await the quarterly delivery numbers. If these numbers meet or exceed expectations, Tesla's stock enjoys a nice, steady climb, akin to a gentle hike up a scenic mountain trail. Conversely, if the numbers disappoint, the stock might take a mild dip, much like that feeling when you realize you forgot your sunscreen.

July and August, on the other hand, often see the stock coasting along, reflecting a period of consolidation where investors are content to sit back and sip their iced tea. However, it's not just a time for relaxation, but also for reassessment and strategic planning. As the market digests the mid-year financials and looks forward to the year's second half, this strategic pause in the summer can be a valuable opportunity for investors to prepare for potential market shifts and position themselves for the future.

Market Influences in Summer

But what external factors contribute to summer stability? Let's examine them.

Economic Indicators

The broader economy significantly influences Tesla's stock performance during the summer. Economic data such as employment figures, GDP growth, and consumer confidence can bolster or undermine investor sentiment. When the economy is doing well, investors are more likely to feel optimistic about

The Secret to Tesla's Stock Market Success

high-growth stocks like Tesla, leading to steady or slightly rising prices.

Earnings Reports

Tesla typically releases its Q2 earnings report in late July. This report is a pivotal moment in the summer cycle, often causing short-term fluctuations based on performance metrics such as revenue, net income, and future guidance. A strong earnings report can be like finding an extra scoop of ice cream in your cone, sweetening the summer even more.

Regulatory News

Any updates on regulations affecting the automotive or energy sectors can sway Tesla's stock. For instance, announcements about subsidies for electric vehicles or new environmental policies can provide a boost, much like a surprise summer thunderstorm that cools things down in a good way. Conversely, negative regulatory news can dampen the mood and the stock.

Market Sentiment

The overall mood of the stock market, often influenced by global events, can also impact Tesla's stock. Geopolitical tensions, trade agreements, or even significant companies' earnings reports can create ripples that reach Tesla. Think of it as the stock market's version of a sudden downpour at a summer picnic—sometimes it's expected, sometimes it's not.

Technological Innovations and Announcements

While significant product launches are rare in the summer, Tesla may still make announcements about technological advancements or new partnerships. Like a pop-up summer concert, these can create buzz and attract investor interest.

Consumer Trends

Summer also sees varied consumer spending patterns, often influencing Tesla's sales, particularly in the consumer discretionary sector. A surge in road trips might increase interest in electric vehicles. At the same time, high gas prices can push more consumers to consider EVs, indirectly benefiting Tesla.

In conclusion, Tesla's summer stability is a blend of predictable financial patterns and the unpredictable nature of market influences. By understanding these dynamics, investors can navigate the summer months with confidence, enjoying the relative calm and preparing for the more turbulent times that might lie ahead. This understanding provides a sense of security and makes investors feel informed and prepared. So, grab your shades, relax, and watch those market trends—summer might be stable, but it's always interesting.

Autumn Adjustments

As the leaves turn golden and the air grows crisp, Tesla's stock embarks on its transformation journey. Let's analyze the trends and patterns that typically unfold during autumn and how they can be leveraged for financial gain.

September: The Setup

September often serves as a preparatory phase. Investors begin positioning themselves for the final quarter of the year. The release of Tesla's Q3 production and delivery numbers in early October typically sets the stage for what's to come.

October: The Earnings Effect

October is crucial due to the Q3 earnings report. This is Tesla's version of mid-term exams. A strong earnings report can result in a significant stock rally, while a miss can cause a dip. Investors scrutinize revenue growth, profit margins, and delivery forecasts, with each metric influencing the stock's trajectory.

November: The Holiday Hustle

As November rolls in, so does the anticipation for holiday sales. This month, speculative trading often increases as investors try to predict how Tesla will perform during the holiday season. Black Friday and Cyber Monday sales figures, which can indicate specific impact on Tesla's stock, can hint at consumer spending and Tesla's potential end-of-year performance. Any updates on new product deliveries or technological advancements can also sway investor sentiment.

Investor Strategies for Autumn

Navigating Tesla's autumn adjustments requires careful analysis, strategic planning, and good fortune. Here are some strategies to help investors make informed decisions during this dynamic season:

Monitor Key Reports

The Secret to Tesla's Stock Market Success

Monitor Tesla's Q3 production, delivery numbers, and earnings report closely. Pay attention to the headlines and details such as cash flow, R&D expenses, and market expansion plans.

Stay Informed About External Factors

Be aware of broader economic conditions and geopolitical events that could impact Tesla's stock. Interest rates, employment figures, and consumer confidence can influence market sentiment. Additionally, any changes in EV regulations or incentives can directly impact Tesla.

Adopt a Flexible Strategy

Autumn is a time of change, and flexibility is critical. Adopt a flexible strategy by reallocating your portfolio, taking profits, or even buying on dips if the long-term outlook remains positive.

Consider Seasonal Trends

Historically, specific trends repeat themselves. For instance, the anticipation of strong holiday sales can drive the stock up in late November. Use historical data to identify these patterns and align your investment strategy accordingly.

Daluxe Inc.

Diversify Your Portfolio

While Tesla may be a star performer, it's wise to diversify your investments. A balanced portfolio can help mitigate risks, especially during periods of high volatility.

Watch for Technological Announcements

Tesla often reveals updates or new projects in the autumn, which can significantly impact the stock. Whether it's advancements in battery technology, new vehicle prototypes, or improvements in self-driving capabilities, these announcements can create substantial market movement.

Evaluate Long-term Potential

Despite short-term fluctuations, consider Tesla's long-term potential. The company's commitment to innovation, sustainability, and market expansion positions it well for future growth. Investors can confidently navigate the autumn months by staying informed, being flexible, and leveraging historical trends.

The Secret to Tesla's Stock Market Success

Winter Woes and Wins

As the temperatures drop, the market activity heats up, making the winter months an exhilarating time for Tesla's stock. Let's embark on a comprehensive study of how Tesla's stock typically behaves during this pivotal season, a journey that promises to be as thrilling as a winter adventure.

Historically, Tesla's stock performance in the winter months—December, January, and February—has been characterized by significant volatility. Imagine navigating an icy road with ups, downs, and slippery moments. This period often involves investor optimism and caution, driven by end-of-year sales, annual financial reports, and broader market sentiment.

December: The Festive Frenzy

December is a critical month for Tesla, with the holiday season as a significant catalyst for stock movements. The anticipation of strong year-end sales, especially around Black Friday and Christmas, can increase stock prices. Investors are keenly aware that a robust holiday sales performance can set a positive tone for the year ahead.

However, December also brings potential pitfalls. Any sign of missed sales targets or production delays can cause jitters, leading to sharp declines. It's like hanging the perfect Christmas lights display—one misstep, and the whole thing can come crashing down.

January: New Year, New Challenges

January starts the new year with renewed investor optimism and the reality check of Q4 earnings reports. This month often sees heightened activity as investors reassess their portfolios and Tesla's stock reflects the company's year-end performance. If Tesla finishes the year strong, the stock can enjoy a bullish start to the new year. Conversely, negative surprises can lead to a rocky beginning, like New Year's resolutions that start strong but quickly fizzle out.

February: The Mid-Winter Mark

February can be quieter than December and January, but it's far from dull. Investors look forward to Tesla's full-year earnings report, typically released late in the month. This report comprehensively reviews the previous year's performance and provides guidance for the year ahead. Positive results can generate significant upward momentum, while any shortfalls can prompt a reassessment of the stock's value. Think of

The Secret to Tesla's Stock Market Success

February as the Groundhog Day for Tesla's stock—depending on the earnings report, investors might see an early spring (bullish trend) or more winter woes (bearish trend).

Holiday Season Impacts

The holiday season on Tesla's stock is a significant event that holds both potential rewards and risks. This period is marked by increased consumer spending, directly influencing Tesla's sales and, consequently, its stock performance. Let's explore how the holiday season shapes investor sentiment, market value, and the potential rewards and risks it brings, painting a vivid picture of the stakes involved.

The holiday season typically drives consumer spending on big-ticket items, including cars. Tesla often sees a spike in vehicle deliveries and sales during this period, boosting revenue and market confidence. It's like receiving a bonus gift under the tree—unexpected yet delightful.

End-of-Year Discounts and Promotions

Tesla sometimes offers end-of-year incentives to boost sales, such as discounts on existing inventory or favorable financing options. These promotions can lead to a year-end sales rush, further elevating investor confidence and stock prices.

Production and Delivery Targets

Investors keenly watch whether Tesla meets its production and delivery targets. Achieving or exceeding these targets can lead to a rally in stock prices, while any shortfall can result in a decline. It's similar to the anticipation of unwrapping gifts—you hope for the best, but there's always a risk of disappointment.

Annual Financial Reporting

The annual financial report, released in January, provides a comprehensive overview of Tesla's performance, including revenue, profit margins, and future projections. This report significantly impacts investor sentiment, much like a post-holiday review of your credit card statement—it reveals how well you did and what to expect going forward.

Market Sentiment and Broader Economic Trends

During the holiday season, the overall market sentiment plays a crucial role, acting as a psychological driver for Tesla's stock.

The Secret to Tesla's Stock Market Success

Positive economic indicators such as substantial employment and consumer confidence can boost Tesla's stock, while negative news can have the opposite effect. Think of it as the difference between a festive holiday party and a canceled event due to bad weather—the atmosphere makes all the difference.

The winter season presents a double-edged sword for Tesla's stock, with significant activity and volatility. By understanding the trends and patterns of this period, investors can feel empowered to navigate the potential rewards and risks.

Understanding Tesla's seasonal cycles is like mastering winemaking - it requires patience, timing, and knowing when to act. By recognizing these patterns, investors can better navigate the ups and downs, allowing for strategic entry and exit points for trades. Tesla's seasonal behavior offers numerous opportunities to maximize profits. Aligning your investment strategy with these trends will better equip you to capitalize on Tesla's cyclical behavior and celebrate your success.

Daluxe Inc.

Chapter 4: Analyzing Tesla's Financial Health

Quarterly Reports Overview

In the world of investing, quarterly reports are invaluable. Think of them as the backstage pass to Tesla's grand theater, offering an exclusive peek into the inner workings of the company, its performance, and its prospects. As a potential investor, you're being granted access to this privileged information.

Daluxe Inc.

A quarterly report is like a treasure map, with several crucial sections leading you to the heart of Tesla's financial performance. Each piece of this puzzle provides a unique perspective, helping you understand how the company is navigating the market.

Balance Sheet

Imagine this as a snapshot of Tesla's financial health at a specific time. It lists the company's assets, liabilities, and shareholders' equity. Think of it like checking your bank account on payday—hopefully, it's in the black. For Tesla, a robust balance sheet signifies financial stability and the capacity to weather economic storms.

Income Statement

This is where Tesla's performance over a specific period gets dissected. It reveals revenues, expenses, and profits (or losses, as the case may be). Reading an income statement is akin to reading a restaurant review; it tells you how well Tesla serves its electric cars and energy solutions to the hungry market.

The Secret to Tesla's Stock Market Success

Cash Flow Statement

If the income statement is a restaurant review, the cash flow statement is the kitchen tour. It shows where the money is coming from and where it's going. Cash flow is crucial because, as they say, "Cash is king." Positive cash flow means Tesla has more money flowing in than out, indicating financial health and operational efficiency.

Management's Discussion and Analysis (MD&A)

In this section, the executives play storytellers, providing context to the numbers. They discuss the reasons behind the company's performance, strategies for the future, and potential risks. Consider it the director's commentary on Tesla's financial performance—insightful, sometimes a bit boastful, but always essential for understanding the bigger picture.

Why should you invest your time in understanding Tesla's quarterly reports? These reports are the key to unlocking the stock market's secrets and translating complex financial data into practical insights. They empower investors to determine whether Tesla is soaring toward success or veering toward a potential crash.

For instance, a surge in revenue might indicate strong demand for Tesla's vehicles or energy products. But beware! It's crucial to delve deeper, like a well-plotted twist in a thriller. Is the revenue growth sustainable, or is it driven by one-time events? Are there rising costs that might eat into future profits? A thorough analysis of the quarterly report can reveal these subtleties. It's your responsibility as an investor to dig deep and understand the true story behind the numbers.

Similarly, changes in Tesla's cash flow can signal shifts in its operational efficiency. A sudden dip might suggest increased spending on R&D or new factory expansions—investments that could pay off handsomely. Conversely, a consistent negative cash flow could indicate deeper issues, like unsustainable business practices or looming financial troubles.

While quarterly reports may lack the glamor of a blockbuster movie or the wit of a stand-up comedy show, they are indispensable tools for any serious investor. By mastering the art of reading and interpreting these reports, you equip yourself with the knowledge to make informed, strategic decisions.

Key Metrics to Watch

Welcome to the enchanted realm of financial metrics, where numbers dance, and data sings the ballad of Tesla's market performance. Suppose quarterly reports are the script of this grand production. In that case, key metrics are the star actors, each playing a pivotal role in Tesla's financial saga drama.

Revenue Growth

Revenue growth tells the story of Tesla's sales performance, revealing whether the public's appetite for electric cars and solar panels is waxing or waning. Think of it as the box office receipts for Tesla's latest blockbuster. A strong revenue growth is akin to a sold-out opening night, signaling that the audience loves what Tesla offers. Conversely, a dip might suggest that the critics are lukewarm and Tesla's show needs to be more appealing.

Gross Margin

Enter the suave sidekick, ensuring the hero's triumphs are not just fleeting victories. A high gross margin means Tesla is keeping more of each dollar earned, much like a savvy actor negotiating a hefty cut of the box office take. A low gross margin, however, could indicate that costs are eating into profits.

Daluxe Inc.

Operating Expenses

The operating expenses cover the day-to-day costs of running Tesla. This includes everything from research and development (R&D) to marketing and administrative expenses. High operating expenses might suggest that Tesla is investing heavily in future growth—think of it as method acting, pouring everything into the role. But beware if these costs skyrocket without a corresponding rise in revenue, as it could signal that Tesla is throwing money at problems without seeing a return, like a production over budget and behind schedule.

Net Income

The climactic revelation is the moment when all plot threads converge. Net income remains after all expenses are deducted from revenue. It's the final verdict on whether Tesla's latest performance is a blockbuster hit or a box office bomb. Positive net income is the standing ovation, the applause that signifies success. Negative net income, on the other hand, is the dreaded boo from the balcony, indicating that all is not well behind the scenes.

The Secret to Tesla's Stock Market Success

Earnings Per Share (EPS)

EPS divides net income by the number of outstanding shares, giving a per-share profit measure. High EPS is like a glowing review, attracting more investors to the Tesla show. Low EPS, however, might deter potential fans, much like a panned performance keeps audiences away from the theater.

Cash Flow

Cash flow is the cash Tesla generates after accounting for capital expenditures. It's the cash that Tesla has available to invest in new projects, pay down debt, or return to shareholders. Think of it as the behind-the-scenes budget, ensuring that production can keep running smoothly. A healthy FCF means Tesla has the financial flexibility to innovate and expand. Negative FCF, however, could signal that Tesla is burning through cash faster than a pyrotechnics display gone awry.

Debt Levels

Monitor Tesla's debt-to-equity ratio, which compares total debt to shareholders' equity. A high ratio might suggest Tesla is overleveraged, like a production borrowing heavily against

Daluxe Inc.

future ticket sales. A low ratio indicates a more conservative approach, with Tesla maintaining financial stability.

These key metrics shine a spotlight on Tesla's financial stage, illuminate the performance and guide investors through the complex narrative. By watching these metrics closely, you can discern the underlying storylines and make informed decisions about your investment.

Chapter 5: The Role of Innovation

Tesla's Technological Advancements

Tesla is not just a car company; it's a tech company that happens to make cars. Elon Musk and his merry band of engineers constantly push the boundaries of what's possible, making the company as much about Silicon Valley as it is about Motor City. From self-driving cars to cutting-edge battery technology, Tesla's innovations are the stuff of sci-fi dreams.

Autopilot and Full Self-Driving (FSD)

Imagine cruising down the highway, your hands off the wheel, sipping coffee, and reading the morning news while your car does all the work. This isn't a scene from "The Jetsons"; it's the promise of Tesla's Autopilot and Full Self-Driving (FSD) features. These technologies are not just about convenience; they're about revolutionizing how we think about transportation. Every update to Autopilot or FSD sends ripples through the market, with investors eagerly awaiting the next leap toward fully autonomous driving.

Tesla's Car Battery: The Powerhouse Behind the Wheel

When it comes to Tesla, the show's real star isn't just the sleek design or the futuristic Autopilot—it's the battery. Yes, that humble, often overlooked component is the beating heart of every Tesla vehicle, the unsung hero propelling these electric marvels into the future. So, how does Tesla develop these incredible power sources, and is it all done in-house? Let's dive into the electrifying world of Tesla's car batteries with a jolt of humor and academic flair.

The Birth of a Tesla Battery

The Secret to Tesla's Stock Market Success

Creating a Tesla battery is like crafting a fine wine, requiring precision, expertise, and innovation. The journey begins with the design and development of the battery cell, the fundamental building block of Tesla's power systems. Tesla's recent 4680 cell is more extensive, energy-dense, and efficient than its predecessors, promising to supercharge Tesla's performance and range.

But here's where it gets interesting: while Tesla is the mastermind behind the 4680 designs, the production involves a collaborative effort. Think of it as a culinary masterpiece where Tesla is the celebrity chef, but they still rely on top-notch sous-chefs to bring the dish to life.

The Dynamic Duo: Tesla and Panasonic

Tesla has a long-standing partnership with Panasonic, the Japanese electronics giant, to manufacture its batteries. This dynamic duo operates like a well-oiled machine—or, in this case, a well-charged battery. Panasonic handles the production of the battery cells at Tesla's Gigafactory, a sprawling facility that's part factory, part futuristic dreamscape.

While Panasonic is responsible for producing the battery cells, Tesla focuses on assembly and integration. It's like Tesla handed

Panasonic the recipe for the perfect soufflé, and now they're working together to ensure it rises to perfection.

In-House Innovations: The Gigafactory

Tesla isn't just sitting back and letting Panasonic do all the heavy lifting. The company is heavily involved in the process, constantly innovating to improve battery technology. The Gigafactory itself is a testament to Tesla's commitment to pushing boundaries. Here, Tesla and Panasonic collaborate on every aspect of battery production, from raw material sourcing to final assembly.

The Gigafactory aims to reduce costs through economies of scale, bringing down the price of batteries and, by extension, the cost of electric vehicles. This facility is a powerhouse of efficiency.

Beyond Panasonic: Expanding Partnerships

Tesla's ambitions don't stop with Panasonic. The company has partnered with suppliers like LG Chem and CATL to diversify its battery supply chain. It's like Tesla is assembling an all-star team of battery makers, each bringing their unique strengths.

These collaborations help Tesla meet the growing demand for its vehicles and ensure a steady supply of high-quality batteries.

The Future of Tesla Batteries

Looking ahead, Tesla continues to innovate in battery technology. The company is exploring new materials, such as silicon anodes and solid-state batteries, which promise even more significant energy density and safety. Tesla's goal is to create batteries that are more powerful, sustainable, and environmentally friendly.

While Tesla designs and oversees the development of these energy marvels, they partner with industry leaders like Panasonic to bring their vision to life. This symbiotic relationship ensures that every Tesla on the road is powered by cutting-edge technology, driving the future of electric mobility. So, next time you see a Tesla gliding silently down the street, remember that its power source results from a global effort to revolutionize how we drive.

Energy Solutions

Tesla's innovation isn't confined to the open road; it's also reshaping our energy landscape. With products like the

Powerwall, Powerpack, and Solar Roof, Tesla is at the forefront of the renewable energy revolution. These technologies are designed to store and manage energy more efficiently, reducing our reliance on fossil fuels and pushing us toward a more sustainable future. Investors see these advancements as a key to Tesla's long-term growth, providing diverse revenue streams and reinforcing the company's role as a leader in clean energy.

Impact of New Releases

Tesla's new product releases are akin to blockbuster movie premieres, generating buzz, excitement, and sometimes even controversy. Each unveiling is an event, often shrouded in secrecy and speculation, until the big reveal sends shockwaves through the market, leaving investors and enthusiasts alike intrigued about the next big thing.

The Model 3 and Model Y

Remember the frenzy when the Model 3 was announced? It was like the automotive equivalent of a new iPhone launch, with lines forming and pre-orders flying in from around the world. The Model 3's promise of an affordable, mass-market electric car was a game-changer, and its impact on Tesla's stock was profound. Similarly, with its crossover appeal, the Model Y tapped into the ever-growing SUV market, further solidifying Tesla's market position.

The Cybertruck

Then there's the Cybertruck, Tesla's foray into the world of trucks that look like they've driven straight out of a dystopian future. Love it or hate it, the Cybertruck's debut was a masterclass in generating buzz. Its polarizing design and bold performance claims turned heads. They captured headlines, impacting Tesla's stock with the same intensity as a viral meme.

The roboTaxi Concept

Tesla has introduced the concept of roboTaxis, which involves a combination of vehicles owned by the company and privately owned cars. This model is akin to an automotive version of Airbnb, where private individuals can lease their roboTaxis to those interested in experiencing futuristic urban transportation without the burden of car ownership. Tesla's roboTaxi concept underscores its commitment to revolutionizing transportation and establishing a user-focused network of shared vehicles. Additionally, this model presents a novel revenue opportunity for investors by integrating car ownership with the gig economy.

Daluxe Inc.

The RoboVan

The RoboVan is a futuristic, fully electric, self-driving van that's anything but ordinary. Imagine a smooth, minimalist design paired with Tesla's Full Self-Driving (FSD) tech, letting the van handle traffic, park itself, and avoid obstacles while you sip coffee or binge Netflix. Perfect for families, deliveries, or businesses, the RoboVan's spacious, high-tech interior makes multitasking a breeze. Eco-friendly and versatile, it's not just a van—it's a glimpse into the future of transportation, with zero emissions and maximum cool factor.

Optimus

And now, ladies and gentlemen, let's talk about Optimus, Tesla's humanoid robot. No, this isn't a scene from "Transformers," though the name does spark some robotic nostalgia. Optimus is designed to handle mundane tasks, from lifting heavy objects to doing the laundry—essentially the perfect houseguest who never overstays their welcome. But Optimus is more than just a helpful companion. It represents Tesla's foray into robotics for the market, signaling potential new avenues for revenue and innovation. Imagine a future where Tesla powers your car and your home and helps with your chores. Investors are eagerly anticipating this development, as Optimus could open up vast new automation and artificial intelligence markets, further expanding Tesla's reach and influence.

The Secret to Tesla's Stock Market Success

The Ripple Effect

Every new release, every technological advancement, creates a ripple effect that reverberates across the stock market. Investors keenly observe these innovations, viewing them as indicators of Tesla's future performance and market potential. A successful product launch can send Tesla's stock soaring, while production delays or technical hiccups can lead to temporary dips. This direct correlation between innovation and financial performance underscores the pivotal role of Tesla's technological advancements in shaping its market cycles and financial destiny.

Innovation is Tesla's lifeblood, driving its market cycles and shaping its financial destiny. By staying ahead of the technological curve, Tesla sets itself apart from traditional automakers and positions itself as a leader in the broader tech and energy sectors. For investors, your role in keeping a finger on the pulse of Tesla's innovation is crucial for understanding the company's trajectory and making informed decisions, underscoring your value in Tesla's success.

So, as we explore Tesla's technological advancements and new releases, remember that you're not just watching a company grow—you're witnessing the future unfold. Stay tuned, stay curious, and enjoy the show because, with Tesla, the next big breakthrough is always just around the corner.

Daluxe Inc.

Chapter 6: External Influences

Many actors are on stage in the grand theater of Tesla's market performance. Still, external influences lurk in the wings—economic conditions such as the 2008 financial crisis, regulations like the California Zero Emission Vehicle program, and political events like the US-China trade war. These backstage players can sometimes steal the spotlight, dramatically impacting Tesla's seasonal cycles.

Economic Factors

Inflation: The Balloon Effect

Inflation is like a friend who insists on blowing up balloons at a party—eventually, something will pop. When inflation rises, the cost of raw materials and production increases, squeezing Tesla's profit margins. Higher lithium, cobalt, and nickel prices can turn a healthy bottom line into a deflated balloon. Investors need to keep an eye on inflation rates because when the cost of making electric cars rises, so do consumer prices, potentially cooling demand.

Interest Rates: The Yo-Yo Phenomenon

Interest rates are the yo-yo of the financial world—always going up and down. When interest rates are low, borrowing is cheap, and consumers are more likely to finance big purchases like Tesla vehicles. However, when the central banks decide it's time for a rate hike, borrowing becomes more expensive, which can dampen consumer enthusiasm. For Tesla, which often relies on consumers taking out loans to buy their cars, high interest rates can mean fewer sales and a rollercoaster ride for the stock price.

The Secret to Tesla's Stock Market Success

Economic Growth: The Rising Tide

Consumer confidence is high when the economy is booming, and people are more likely to make significant investments, like buying a shiny new Tesla. Conversely, people tighten their belts during economic downturns, and big-ticket items like electric cars may find fewer buyers. Tesla's performance is thus closely tied to the economy's overall health, making it essential for investors to keep an eye on GDP growth and consumer sentiment.

Tesla's Megafactories: The Production Powerhouses

Tesla's six colossal Gigafactories, strategically located in Fremont, California; Sparks, Nevada; Berlin, Germany; Shanghai, China; Austin, Texas; and Buffalo, New York, are not just production powerhouses, but also key players in the global economic landscape. These factories, operating at an impressive pace, are the backbone of Tesla's production, supplying vehicles and energy products to meet the demands of various economies.

Economic Growth

So, what happens to Tesla's revenue if the US, Europe, and China economies are doing well? Well, sit back and imagine this scenario:

A Booming US Economy

In the United States, a booming economy not only signifies consumers' increased disposable income but also their heightened confidence in making significant purchases. This, in turn, leads to a surge in demand for Tesla's vehicles, particularly the more affordable Model 3 and Model Y. With Gigafactories in Fremont, Sparks, Austin, and Buffalo operating at full capacity, Tesla can readily meet this upswing in demand. As sales figures reach unprecedented heights, revenues skyrocket, and the stock price receives a much-welcomed boost, instilling a sense of optimism and hope in investors.

Economic Prosperity in Europe

Across the pond in Europe, a strong economy means more green incentives from governments pushing for electric vehicle adoption. Gigafactory Berlin, Tesla's European stronghold, steps up to the plate. With efficient production and lower shipping costs, Tesla can supply the European market more effectively. Increased sales, driven by consumer demand and

The Secret to Tesla's Stock Market Success

favorable government policies, fill Tesla's coffers, making shareholders smile.

China's Economic Growth

Economic growth in China, the world's largest auto market, spells good news for Tesla. Gigafactory Shanghai, already a powerhouse of production, ramps up even further. The Chinese market's appetite for electric vehicles continues to grow, and with local production reducing costs, Tesla can offer competitive prices. As more Model 3s and Model Ys roll off the production line, Tesla's revenue from the Asian market skyrockets.

The Combined Effect

Tesla's revenue sees a significant uptick, with all three major economies firing on all cylinders. The increased demand from these robust economies ensures that Tesla's Gigafactories operate at total capacity, maximizing efficiency and profitability. Investors rejoice as quarterly reports show record-breaking revenues, and Tesla's position as a market leader solidifies even further.

In conclusion, when the US, European, and Chinese economies are thriving, Tesla's revenue experiences a delightful surge.

Increased consumer spending, favorable government policies, and efficient production capabilities propel Tesla to new financial heights.

Economic Downturn

Now, let's flip the script. What happens if the US, Europe, and China economies take a nosedive? Grab your popcorn because this could be a drama with severe twists and turns.

Economic Downturn in the US

When the US economy stumbles, consumers swiftly tighten their belts, often delaying big purchases like cars. This could put Tesla, with its high-end models, in a challenging position. A decrease in consumer spending could lead to fewer people investing in the latest Model S or Model Y. Gigafactories in Fremont, Sparks, Austin, and Buffalo might experience production slowdowns, resulting in lower revenues and potential layoffs. The stock price could also be affected as investors prepare for potential lower sales and profits.

European Economic Woes

The Secret to Tesla's Stock Market Success

Across the Atlantic, a struggling European economy could spell trouble for Tesla's Berlin Gigafactory. Europe has been a stronghold for electric vehicle adoption, but an economic downturn could shift priorities. Government subsidies for EVs might be reduced or eliminated, and consumers might opt for cheaper, conventional vehicles. Reduced demand means lower production, hitting Tesla's bottom line and causing a ripple effect that could drag down the stock price. Investors might panic, fearing that the once-booming European market is drying up.

China's Economic Slump

If China's economy hits the skids, it's like watching a slow-motion car crash. China is Tesla's largest market outside the US, and any economic turbulence there can have a massive impact. Gigafactory Shanghai, Tesla's production powerhouse, might face reduced demand, leading to overcapacity and inefficiencies. Trade tensions and tariffs could exacerbate the situation, increasing costs and squeezing margins. Sales plummet, revenue drops and the stock price could nosedive as investors flee to safer havens.

The Combined Catastrophe

If all three major economies were to experience a downturn, Tesla would face a formidable challenge. A global decrease in demand would necessitate a reduction in Tesla's production, leading to higher per-unit costs and lower profit margins. The resulting financial strain could force Tesla to postpone or scale back new projects, potentially impacting future growth prospects. Investors would likely react with concern, causing the stock price to decline as confidence in Tesla's ability to navigate the economic turbulence diminishes.

Conclusion: A Tale of Two Economies

Economic factors, regulatory landscapes, and political events are key players in Tesla's market performance drama. Whether basking in the glow of a booming global economy or weathering the storm of economic downturns, Tesla's fortunes are intricately tied to the broader economic environment. It's crucial for investors and stakeholders to remain vigilant, monitoring economic indicators and geopolitical developments to anticipate the twists and turns in Tesla's journey. This emphasis on staying informed and engaged can help individuals feel more connected to Tesla's market performance.

Therefore, it is essential for you to maintain a watchful eye on the broader economic trends, regulatory changes, and political landscape. In the dynamic theater of Tesla's market performance, these external influences are unpredictable elements that can swiftly alter the course.

Regulatory and Political Impacts

While economic factors are like the weather—sometimes predictable but often capricious—regulatory and political impacts are more like puppet masters, pulling strings behind the scenes. These influences can profoundly affect Tesla's market performance, shaping the landscape in which it operates.

Environmental Regulations: The Green Light

Environmental regulations, the green light in Tesla's world, propelling the company forward. Governments worldwide are tightening emissions standards and promoting electric vehicles through subsidies and tax incentives. These regulations can significantly influence Tesla's market performance and your investment returns.

Trade Policies: The Tightrope Walk

Trade policies can make or break Tesla's global strategy. Tariffs on imported goods, trade wars, and shifting international relations can all impact Tesla's supply chain and production costs. For example, tariffs on Chinese-made components can increase production costs for Tesla's American factories. Conversely, favorable trade agreements can open up new markets and reduce costs. Tesla must constantly balance on this tightrope, adapting to changes in trade policies to maintain its competitive edge.

Political Climate: The Wild Card

Politics, the unpredictable element in the deck of external influences. Political events and decisions can have immediate and far-reaching effects on Tesla's market performance. A sudden change in government policy, new legislation, or international agreements can either boost or hinder Tesla's operations. Stay alert, as these political shifts can significantly impact your investment strategy.

Elections, geopolitical tensions, and legislative changes are all part of the political climate that Tesla must navigate. Investors should pay attention to political developments because they can lead to swift changes in market conditions, creating both opportunities and risks for Tesla.

Conclusion: The Grand Ensemble

Economic factors, regulatory landscapes, and political events are the grand ensemble cast in Tesla's market performance drama. Keep your eyes on the broader economic trends by following key economic indicators, stay informed about regulatory changes through official government channels and industry news, and watch the political stage closely by tracking political developments and their potential impact on Tesla. In the ever-evolving theater of Tesla's market performance, these external influences are the unpredictable elements that can instantly turn the tide.

Daluxe Inc.

Chapter 7: Case Studies

Welcome to the Hall of Fame and Infamy of Tesla Investments! Here, we'll embark on a thrilling case study that underscores the excitement of considering internal, external, and seasonal factors before buying Tesla stock. Get ready for a ride that includes exhilarating success stories and a few cautionary tales.

How to Get Tesla's Quarterly Report and How to Analyze It

So, you're about to embark on an exhilarating journey into the world of Tesla, the stock market's thrilling roller coaster. As you gear up for this adventure, one crucial tool in your investor's arsenal is Tesla's quarterly report. But how do you lay your hands on this coveted document, and more importantly, how do you decipher its secrets? Let's plunge into the depths of this guide.

Step 1: Empowering Yourself with the Sacred Scroll (Ahem, Quarterly Report)

Tesla's quarterly reports are like hidden treasures, leading you to potential wealth. Here's where you can unearth them:

1. **Tesla Investor Relations Website**: The most direct source. Simply navigate to Tesla Investor Relations at <https://ir.tesla.com/#quarterly-disclosure> where you can find all the latest reports under the "Financials" section.
2. **SEC Filings**: For those who enjoy a bit of formality, the U.S. Securities and Exchange Commission (SEC) hosts Tesla's filings. Head to the SEC's EDGAR database at <https://www.sec.gov/edgar/search-and-access> and search for Tesla.
3. **Financial News Websites**: Sites like Nasdaq, Yahoo Finance, and MarketWatch also post summaries and links to Tesla's reports.

Step 2: Unraveling the Mysteries of the Quarterly Report

Once you have the report, it's time to decode its secrets. Here's a step-by-step guide to analyzing Tesla's quarterly report:

The Executive Summary

Start with the executive summary, which offers a high-level overview of Tesla's performance. This section includes highlights of revenue, net income, and significant achievements. Think of it as the "previously on Tesla" recap.

Financial Statements

Next, dive into the financial statements. Don't worry; they're not as complex as they seem. These are the heart of the report:

- **Income Statement**: Shows revenue, expenses, and profit over the quarter. Look for trends in revenue growth and net income.
- **Balance Sheet**: This list includes assets, liabilities, and shareholders' equity. You can check Tesla's financial health by examining its cash reserves and debt levels.

- **Cash Flow Statement**: This statement reveals cash inflows and outflows.

Key Metrics

Pay special attention to key metrics that drive Tesla's performance:

- **Revenue Growth**: Is Tesla selling more cars and energy products?
- **Gross Margin**: Indicates how efficiently Tesla is turning revenue into profit.
- **Net Income**: The bottom line is how much profit is left after all expenses.

Case Study: The Comprehensive Investor – Sarah's Journey

In this case study, we will follow Sarah, a meticulous investor, as she navigates the complex world of Tesla stock investment. Sarah's journey is a testament to the importance of thorough research and analysis in making successful investment decisions.

Internal Factors

The Secret to Tesla's Stock Market Success

Sarah starts by examining Tesla's internal metrics. She dives into quarterly reports, paying close attention to key metrics such as revenue growth, gross margins, operating expenses, and net income. For instance, she looks at Tesla's revenue trend.

Revenue Growth

With her love for numbers and a touch of drama, Sarah decides to present Tesla's exciting revenue growth versus estimates in a table. It's like a scene from a financial mystery, where each cell in the table reveals a clue to the larger story of Tesla's performance.

Tesla Revenue Growth vs. Estimates

Quarter	Actual Revenue (in billions)	Estimated Revenue (in billions)	Outcome
Q1 2022	18.76	18.1	Exceeded by $0.66 billion
Q2 2022	16.93	17.1	Missed by $0.17 billion
Q3 2022	21.45	21.96	Missed by $0.51 billion
Q4 2022	24.32	24.16	Exceeded by $0.16 billion
Q1 2023	23.33	23.1	Exceeded by $0.23 billion
Q2 2023	24.93	24.72	Exceeded by $0.21 billion
Q3 2023	25.71	25.8	Missed by $0.09 billion
Q4 2023	28.32	28.2	Exceeded by $0.12 billion

Daluxe Inc.

In Q1 2022, Tesla reported a revenue of $18.76 billion, slightly above the estimated $18.10 billion. "A neat little overtake," Sarah notes with a grin.

By Q2 2022, the revenue hit $16.93 billion, just a whisker away from the $17.10 billion estimate. "A close shave," she chuckles, picturing a car barely missing a turn.

Q3 2022 saw revenue at $21.45 billion, compared to the $21.96 billion forecast—a slight dip, but still an impressive sprint. "Tesla might have taken a pit stop," she muses.

Q4 2022 rounded off with $24.32 billion, overtaking the $24.16 billion estimate—another win in Tesla's book.

Fast forward to 2023, and Sarah's excitement grows. Q1 shows Tesla smashing the $23.10 billion estimate with a reported $23.33 billion. This dramatic increase in revenue is sure to keep the audience engaged.

In Q2 2023, Tesla posted $24.93 billion in revenue, comfortably surpassing the $24.72 billion estimate.

The Secret to Tesla's Stock Market Success

Q3 2023's revenue clocked in at $25.71 billion against an estimated $25.80 billion—slightly under, but still a commendable run. And Q4 2023 ended with a roaring $28.32 billion, outpacing the $28.20 billion forecast.

Sarah steps back to admire the trend: Tesla has consistently flirted with estimates, sometimes coming up just short but more often than not exceeding expectations. It's a dance of numbers, a ballet of financial performance. This inspiring growth is like a well-tuned electric engine—powerful, smooth, and full of surprises. It's a testament to Tesla's potential, and the audience can't help but feel optimistic about the company's future.

Comparing Tesla's revenue growth versus estimates over the past two years paints a picture of a company that thrives on keeping analysts on their toes. "In the grand race of corporate earnings," she thinks, "Tesla is definitely in the lead, and it's one thrilling ride to watch."

Daluxe Inc.

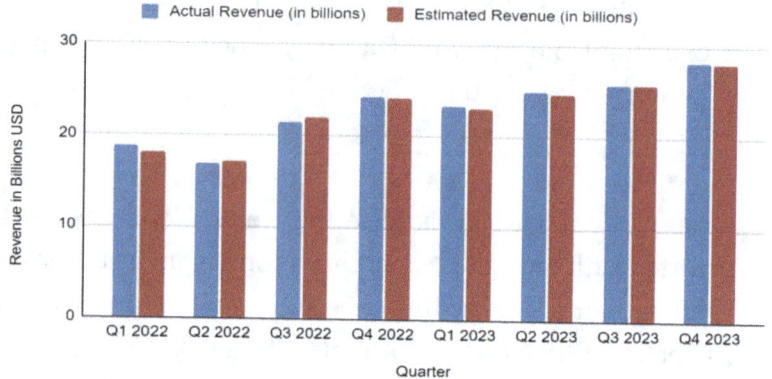

Analyzing Tesla's Q1 2024 Report and Comparing it to Q4 2023

Next, Sarah embarks on another financial adventure. This time, she compares Tesla's quarterly revenue, net income, gross margin, and free cash flow.

Tesla's Q1 2024 Report Highlights:

- **Revenue**: $21.30 billion (down from $23.33 billion in Q1 2023)
- **Gross Margin**: 18.5% (excluding regulatory credits)
- **Net Income**: $1.13 billion (down from $2.51 billion in Q1 2023)
- **Free Cash Flow**: -$2.5 billion

The Secret to Tesla's Stock Market Success

Tesla's Q4 2023 Report Highlights:

- **Revenue**: $24.32 billion
- Gross Margin: 20.1%
- **Net Income**: $2.44 billion
- **Free Cash Flow**: $1.1 billion

Now, let's put these numbers into a visual context with a comparison chart:

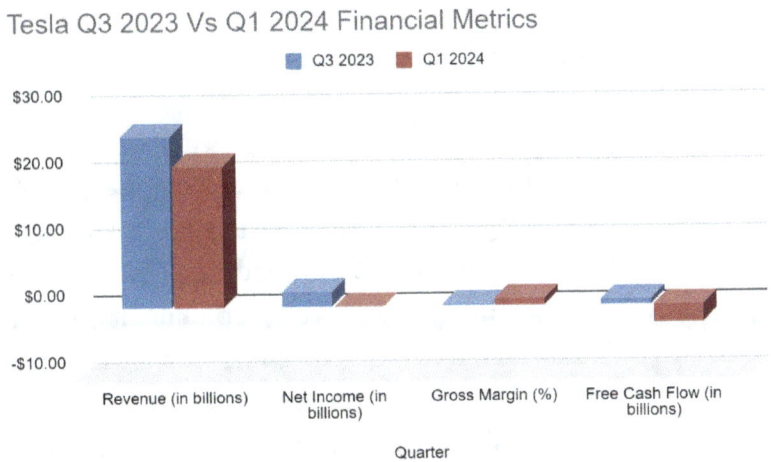

Financial Metrics Comparison

Daluxe Inc.

1. Revenue:
   - Q4 2023: $24.32 billion
   - Q1 2024: $21.30 billion
2. Gross Margin (%):
   - Q4 2023: 20.1%
   - Q1 2024: 18.5%
3. Net Income:
   - Q4 2023: $2.44 billion
   - Q1 2024: $1.13 billion
4. Free Cash Flow:
   - Q4 2023: $1.1 billion
   - Q1 2024: -$2.5 billion

Analysis of the Comparison Chart

1. **Revenue**: Revenue is the lifeblood of any company. In Q4 2023, Tesla's revenue was a healthy $24.32 billion. However, by Q1 2024, it had dipped to $21.30 billion. Despite fluctuations, Tesla still maintains impressive multi-billion-dollar revenues, showing continued strength for future growth.
2. **Gross Margin**: This metric shows the efficiency of turning revenue into profit. In Q4 2023, Tesla's gross margin was 20.1%. By Q1 2024, it dropped slightly to 18.5%. It's not a massive fall, but it is enough to make us wonder if the cost of all those futuristic innovations is catching up.

3. **Net Income**: The bottom line. Q4 2023 saw a robust $2.44 billion, while Q1 2024 reported a much leaner $1.13 billion. Perhaps Tesla spent too much on their Cybertruck redesign or Elon Musk's latest Optimus and roboVan endeavors.
4. **Free Cash Flow**: This is the cash available after all expenses. Q4 2023 was a cozy $1.1 billion, but Q1 2024 drastically dropped to -$2.5 billion. Ouch! Tesla may have invested heavily in new projects or faced unexpected costs.

Conclusion: A Data-Driven Decision

So, what do these numbers tell us? Let's break it down:

- **Revenue and Net Income**: Both metrics declined in Q1 2024 compared to Q4 2023. This could be due to seasonal variations, lower delivery volumes, or strategic price adjustments.
- **Gross Margin**: The gross margin decreased slightly, indicating potential challenges in maintaining profitability.
- **Free Cash Flow**: The sharp drop to negative free cash flow in Q1 2024 is a red flag, suggesting cash flow management issues.

Daluxe Inc.

While Tesla's current financials show some challenges, the company's innovative edge and potential for future growth remain strong. As always, weigh the risks and rewards before making your decision.

Tesla's Technological Development

When Elon Musk talks about Tesla's future, it's like listening to a sci-fi author pitching the next blockbuster saga. In this narrative, the stars are the roboTaxi, the Optimus Bot, and the real-world AI that powers them, transforming Tesla from a car manufacturer into a tech titan of unprecedented scale.

roboTaxi: The Autonomous Anthem

Imagine this: You step out of your house, summon a car with your phone, and moments later, a sleek Tesla Model 3 arrives at your doorstep. There's no driver – just an empty seat waiting for you.

The roboTaxi fleet is Tesla's vision of a fully autonomous ride-hailing service. These vehicles will operate without drivers, relying entirely on Tesla's advanced Full Self-Driving (FSD) system. The FSD, a testament to Tesla's AI prowess, allows the car to navigate streets, avoid obstacles, and deliver you safely to

The Secret to Tesla's Stock Market Success

your destination. For the urban commuter, this means no more parking hassles, no more insurance costs, and no more dealing with that awkward Uber driver small talk. Just smooth, efficient rides whenever you need them.

Example:

Imagine Sarah, a busy New York executive who used to spend hours commuting and hundreds of dollars a month on car expenses. With roboTaxi, she now zips through traffic, using the time to catch up on work or simply relax. Her monthly transport costs have plummeted, and her productivity has soared. Multiply Sarah's experience by millions of users worldwide, and it's easy to see how this could send Tesla's revenue – and stock price – into orbit. This is the kind of future that Tesla's innovations promise, a future that is not just efficient, but also transformative for individuals like Sarah.

Optimus Bot: The Mechanical Maestro

Tesla's humanoid robot, Optimus, is designed to tackle the tedious tasks that we all dislike. Need your house cleaned? Optimus can handle it. Laundry piling up? Optimus is there to help. This isn't just a fancy Roomba; it's a versatile, intelligent assistant capable of managing various household chores. Imagine having a personal assistant who never complains, never takes a day off, and can lift heavy boxes effortlessly. That's the promise of the Optimus Bot.

Example:

Consider John, a busy parent juggling work and family responsibilities. With Optimus Bot, he no longer has to worry about household chores. The robot handles everything from cleaning the kitchen to helping his kids with homework. John now has more time to spend with his family, making his life significantly easier. For Tesla, selling millions of these bots could mean a massive new revenue stream, increasing the stock price.

Tesla AI: The Real-World Genius

At the heart of roboTaxi and Optimus Bot is Tesla's real-world AI. This sophisticated system isn't just a theoretical concept; it's a practical tool that learns and adapts from real-world data. Unlike traditional AI systems that rely on controlled environments, Tesla's AI is honed in the chaotic, unpredictable real world. This makes it exceptionally robust and capable of handling a wide range of tasks with minimal human intervention.

The Secret to Tesla's Stock Market Success

Example:

Imagine a lively city street with people walking, biking, and cars moving smoothly. Tesla's advanced technology helps navigate through this busy environment, ensuring safety and efficiency for everyone. This technology also powers Optimus Bot, which can handle various tasks around the house. Tesla's remarkable adaptability and intelligence sets it apart, making it a crucial element for its future success.

Connecting the Dots: roboTaxi, Optimus Bot, and Tesla's real-world AI

When you connect the dots among roboTaxi, RoboVan, Optimus Bot, and Tesla's real-world AI, you see a company poised for explosive growth. These innovations represent not just technological advancements, but also new revenue streams that could potentially dwarf Tesla's car sales. As these technologies roll out and scale up, the financial impact on Tesla's stock price could be monumental.

In conclusion, Tesla's future is not just a thrilling technological innovation saga, but a potential game-changer in the world of transportation and technology. With roboTaxi, Optimus Bot, and cutting-edge AI, Tesla is not just revolutionizing transportation, but also redefining our relationship with technology. This is a narrative that technology enthusiasts are eagerly watching, ready to witness and be a part of Tesla's next giant leap into the future.

Tesla's Inner Circle's Fighting for Control

In the latest episode of the Tesla saga, a drama unfolded that had all the makings of a corporate thriller. The ongoing saga of Tesla and Elon Musk's compensation package took a fascinating turn in late 2023, with different states in the US showing contrasting attitudes towards the matter. So, buckle up as we take a humorous journey through the peculiar landscape of shareholder votes and state regulations, and explore the implications of these contrasting attitudes.

California: The Golden State's Verdict

Justice Kathleen McCormick found that Tesla's board members were more like Elon Musk's fan club than independent overseers. According to her findings, the board lacked the independence to negotiate Musk's 2018 compensation package at arm's length. Instead of a robust negotiation, it seemed like a starstruck group agreeing to whatever the rock star CEO proposed. For instance, they approved a compensation package that was significantly higher than industry standards without sufficient justification.

The Secret to Tesla's Stock Market Success

Failure to Negotiate at Arm's Length: The Rubber Stamp Routine

In an ideal world, a company's board would counterbalance its CEO, negotiating terms that are fair and in the best interests of shareholders. However, in this case, it appears that the board members were more like rubber stamps than negotiators.

Justice McCormick found that they didn't engage in the rigorous, arm's-length bargaining that would typically accompany a compensation package of such magnitude. It was less a tough negotiation and more a case of 'whatever you say, Elon.'

Keeping Shareholders in the Dark: The Missing Full Picture

But the plot thickens. The judge also highlighted that the board failed to give shareholders the whole picture before asking them to vote on Musk's lavish pay plan. It's like asking someone to invest in a movie without showing the script. The shareholders weren't provided all the critical information they needed to make an informed decision, which is a fundamental aspect of corporate governance. This lack of information could have led to shareholders voting in favor of a compensation plan that was not in their best interests, potentially affecting the company's financial health and their own investments.

Daluxe Inc.

The Texas Advantage: Why the State Might Triumph

Here's where it gets interesting: Texas could play a pivotal role in this saga with its business-friendly environment and enthusiastic support for Musk. Texas is known for its laissez-faire approach to corporate governance, where shareholder votes carry significant weight. If Musk can secure a decisive vote in favor of his compensation package in Texas, it could set a powerful precedent that might influence the outcome across other states.

While a court decision is legally binding, the influence of shareholder votes on corporate policy and decision-making cannot be underestimated. Musk's call for a shareholder vote in Texas is a strategic move to demonstrate the strong support for his compensation package among Tesla's owners.

Elon Musk's call for a shareholder meeting to override the California court's decision is not just a bold move, but a strategic one. By leveraging the enthusiastic support of shareholders in states like Texas, Musk is aiming to demonstrate strong backing for his leadership and compensation package. This battle between judicial rulings and shareholder democracy is a testament to the intricate interplay of governance, legal standards, and corporate strategy.

The Secret to Tesla's Stock Market Success

The Outcome: The Votes are In

When the dust settled, the results were in Musk's favor, but not without a significant number of dissenters. The majority of shareholders voted to maintain the compensation package, doubling down on their belief in Musk's ability to deliver. It was a resounding vote of confidence, echoing the sentiment, "In Musk, we trust." However, the vocal minority who opposed the package made it clear that accountability and fiscal prudence are crucial to Tesla's long-term success. This divergence of opinions is a testament to the complexity of corporate governance.

However, the significant minority who voted against the package clearly stated that accountability and fiscal prudence remain critical to Tesla's long-term success. This diverse range of opinions reminded me that even rock stars need to justify their extravagant riders, and that the path to consensus is only sometimes straightforward.

Connecting the Dots: Shareholder Democracy vs. Judicial Oversight

This scenario underscores the dynamic tension between shareholder democracy and judicial oversight. On one hand, courts ensure that corporate governance standards are upheld and executives are held accountable. On the other hand, shareholder votes represent the voice of the company's owners, who have the right to support or reject management decisions.

The Legality of the Process: A Tale of Two States

The legality of these processes is intricately tied to state-specific corporate governance laws and the principles of shareholder democracy. In California, the legal challenge was rooted in concerns of excessive compensation and fiduciary duty. The court's role was to ensure the package was approved through proper channels and aligned with the shareholders' interests. The judge's ruling underscored that as long as the compensation was approved transparently and legally, it could stand, even if it seemed extravagant.

The legal process was more straightforward in Texas. Corporate governance there emphasizes shareholder votes and the business judgment rule, which protects executive decisions if they are in the best interest of the company and its shareholders. The overwhelming vote favoring Musk's package reflected this trust in Musk's leadership and the belief that high performance justifies high rewards.

The Broader Implications: A Dance of Governance

This vote served as a stark reminder of the delicate balance between rewarding visionary leadership and maintaining corporate governance. For Tesla, it highlighted the challenge of keeping its dynamic CEO motivated while addressing investor concerns. It's akin to managing a high-energy rock band – you want to inspire the lead singer, but you also need to ensure the tour bus stays on the road. This delicate dance is crucial to Tesla's journey toward its ambitious goals.

In conclusion, the recent tussle over Elon Musk's compensation package was a gripping chapter in Tesla's ongoing saga. It showcased the dynamic interplay between visionary leadership and shareholder oversight, reminding everyone that even in Tesla's high-flying world, the principles of good governance still apply. As the company hurtles towards its ambitious goals, investors will watch closely, ready to cast their votes and ensure the Tesla rocket stays on course.

External Factors: Economic and Regulatory Environment

Next, Sarah turns to external factors, recognizing that Tesla's fortunes are tied to broader economic conditions and regulatory landscapes. She consults data from reputable government sources like the Bureau of Economic Analysis (BEA) and the International Monetary Fund (IMF).

Daluxe Inc.

Economic Growth and Inflation: US, Europe, and China in Q1 2024

Sarah examines the GDP growth rates for the US, Europe, and China, noting a mixed bag of recovery post-pandemic. She finds that inflation rates are rising, which could increase production costs and affect consumer purchasing power. These economic factors are important to consider as they can influence Tesla's sales and profitability.

GDP Growth Rates

- United States: The US economy expanded at an annualized rate of 1.6% in Q1 2024, a significant drop from 3.4% in Q4 2023 (IMF, 2024).
- Europe: The Eurozone's GDP grew by approximately 1.2% in Q1 2024, showing a modest recovery but still teetering on the edge of recession (BEA, 2024).
- China: China's GDP grew by 4.6% in Q1 2024, maintaining momentum despite ongoing property sector woes (Neufeld, 2024).

Interest Rates

- United States: The Federal Reserve maintained interest rates at 4.5%, focusing on taming inflation without stifling growth (BEA, 2024).
- Europe: The European Central Bank (ECB) kept its rates at a low 1.5%, balancing between stimulating growth and controlling inflation (BEA, 2024).
- China: The People's Bank of China (PBoC) kept interest rates relatively low at 3.5% to support economic activity amid domestic challenges (Neufeld, 2024).

Inflation Rates

United States: 2.6%

In Q1 2024, the United States maintained a stable inflation rate of 2.6%. This moderate level results from the Federal Reserve's prudent monetary policies and a gradual return to pre-pandemic demand. The US economy is going for a steady jog, ensuring control over inflation without stagnation.

Europe: 3.2%

Over in Europe, the inflation rate for Q1 2024 was slightly higher at 3.2%. The Eurozone has been making this inflation rate feel like a journey on one of those charming but unpredictable

European trains. It's on track, but you might encounter a few delays and price bumps along the way.

China: 1.9%

China, in contrast, reported a modest inflation rate of 1.9% in Q1 2024. The country's economy needs to navigate faster growth and ongoing issues in its property sector. Yet, it has managed to keep inflation relatively low. Picture the Chinese economy as a prudent dragon, moving steadily and responsibly without igniting the world with high prices.

Regulatory Policies

Sarah also looks into government incentives for electric vehicles, which are crucial for Tesla's growth. She notes supportive policies in the US (EV tax credits), Europe (green subsidies), and China (EV purchase incentives), which bode well for Tesla's market potential. Additionally, she considers geopolitical factors such as trade tensions and international relations, which could affect Tesla's global operations and sales.

United States: EV Tax Credits – The Financial Fairy Godmother in Action

EV tax credits have been a game-changer for Tesla and its customers in the US. Imagine this: You're eyeing a sleek Tesla Model 3, but the price seems like a distant dream. Then, the EV tax credit empowers you with a $7,500 reduction. Suddenly, that dream car is within reach, and you feel like the master of your financial destiny.

These tax credits are like a secret weapon for Tesla, making their vehicles more attractive to a broader audience. The increased affordability leads to a surge in sales, and consequently, Tesla's stock price experiences a magical lift. It's a win-win, with the fairy godmother tax credit making dreams come true for buyers and investors.

United States: The Nevada Gigafactory – Subsidies and the American Dream

In the US, Tesla's Gigafactory in Nevada is a shining example of how government subsidies can supercharge a company's growth. In 2014, Tesla struck a deal with the state of Nevada that was more electrifying than a Vegas show. Nevada offered Tesla a package worth a whopping $1.3 billion in subsidies over 20 years. This package included tax breaks, discounted electricity rates, and other incentives.

For Tesla, this was like hitting the jackpot on the slot machine of business opportunities. The subsidies helped fund the construction and operation of the Gigafactory, which produces batteries for Tesla vehicles and energy storage products. As a result, Tesla was able to scale up its production capacity and reduce costs, giving its stock price a jolt akin to a shot of espresso. Filled by the potential for increased production and profitability, investors responded enthusiastically, driving the stock upward.

Europe: Green Subsidies – The Environmental Maestro's Masterpiece

In Europe, green subsidies are orchestrating a symphony of sustainability. For instance, Germany offers EV buyers up to €9,000 in incentives. Imagine a German family choosing between a gas-guzzler and a Tesla Model Y. The subsidies effectively lower Tesla's cost, tipping the scales in favor of the electric option. This not only benefits the environment but also gives the buyers a sense of empowerment, knowing they are contributing to a greener future – all while saving some euros.

Tesla, playing the first chair in this environmental orchestra, enjoys the crescendo of increased sales and market share. As green subsidies amplify across Europe, Tesla's stock price performs a symphonic ascent, hitting high notes that delight investors. It's as if Beethoven himself composed a financial ode to joy for Tesla shareholders.

Europe: The Berlin Gigafactory – A Symphony of Subsidies

Over in Europe, Tesla's Gigafactory Berlin, or "Giga Berlin" as it's fondly known, is another testament to the power of government subsidies. The German government, keen to promote green technology and boost local employment, offered Tesla incentives amounting to nearly €1 billion. This support included grants, tax breaks, and subsidies for research and development.

In July 2024, Tesla received approval to expand its Gigafactory Berlin, aiming to increase production capacity to potentially 1 million vehicles annually. The expansion includes new storage facilities, a battery cell test lab, and improved logistics areas.

Imagine Tesla as a rock band on its European tour, receiving VIP treatment at every stop. The market, witnessing Tesla's expanding footprint and the German government's backing, responded like fans at a sold-out concert – with roaring approval, pushing Tesla's stock to new heights.

Daluxe Inc.

China: EV Purchase Incentives – The Economic Dragon's Fiery Boost

In China, EV purchase incentives breathe fire into the market with formidable force. For example, the Chinese government offers a subsidy of up to ¥25,000 for new energy vehicles. A potential Tesla Model 3 buyer in Shanghai might find the car's price substantially reduced thanks to these incentives. It's like finding a treasure chest at the end of the dragon's fiery trail—irresistible and rewarding.

For Tesla, these incentives are a catalyst for market dominance. Like a mythical dragon, the company's sales figures in China soar, propelling its stock price on powerful updrafts of investor confidence. The incentives reshape the market landscape, positioning Tesla as the reigning champion in the EV kingdom.

China: The Shanghai Gigafactory – The Dragon's Golden Treasure

In China, Tesla's Gigafactory Shanghai, or "Giga Shanghai," illustrates how government support can transform a company's fortunes. When Tesla decided to build its factory in Shanghai, the Chinese government rolled out the red carpet, offering a range of incentives. These included a loan of approximately $1.6 billion from local banks, facilitated land grants, and tax breaks.

The Secret to Tesla's Stock Market Success

Tesla entered the Chinese market like a blockbuster movie premiere, with fireworks. The subsidies allowed Tesla to quickly establish and ramp up production, making the Shanghai factory one of its most productive and cost-efficient. This strategic move enabled Tesla to cater to the burgeoning Chinese EV market, significantly boosting sales. Always eager for a good plot twist, the stock market reacted positively, sending Tesla's shares soaring like a dragon taking flight.

Connecting the Dots: The Global Symphony of Tesla's Stock Price

When we connect these policy dots, the result is a global symphony where Tesla's stock price dances to the tunes of supportive fiscal, environmental, and economic policies. US tax credits ensure that financial barriers melt away, Europe's green subsidies create an environment of sustainability, and China's purchase incentives ignite market fervor.

For the buyers, these policies transform the once-daunting prospect of purchasing an EV into a practical and appealing choice. These benefits, coupled with the increase in sales that drives Tesla's stock price upward, create a virtuous cycle of growth and innovation, making Tesla an attractive investment option for potential buyers.

Daluxe Inc.

The US subsidies for the Nevada Gigafactory laid the foundation for large-scale battery production. Europe's support for Giga Berlin has bolstered Tesla's presence and production capacity. Meanwhile, China's incentives for Giga Shanghai have ensured that Tesla remains a dominant player in the world's largest EV market.

For Tesla, these subsidies are like receiving VIP passes to the hottest events in town, ensuring smooth operations and rapid expansion. For investors, these government-backed incentives translate into robust growth prospects and, consequently, a rising stock price.

In conclusion, the US, Europe, and China subsidies have been instrumental in Tesla's global success, making the company's journey as thrilling and impactful as a headlining act on a world tour.

The symphony of supportive policies from the US, Europe, and China compose a harmonious concerto that elevates Tesla's stock price and significantly contributes to its market success. It's a performance where everyone gets a standing ovation – Tesla, its customers, and the environment. This underscores the crucial role of supportive policies in Tesla's growth and market success, a fact that potential investors should consider.

Seasonal Factors

Sarah doesn't stop at internal and external factors; she also considers seasonal trends. For example, she observes that Tesla's stock often experiences volatility around product launches and financial report releases.

Seasonal Trends

Spring and summer tend to be periods of growth for Tesla due to new product announcements and delivery reports. Conversely, autumn and winter might see more fluctuations due to year-end financial adjustments and profit-taking.

For example, Sarah notes that Tesla's stock often experiences a surge in spring due to the excitement around new vehicle launches, and a dip in autumn as investors take profits before the end of the year.

The Decision: A Well-Informed Investment

With comprehensive data, Sarah decides to invest in Tesla during a spring surge, anticipating positive quarterly reports and new product announcements. She sets a target to review her investment quarterly, ensuring she adapts to any economic or internal performance changes.

Analysis of Investing in Tesla

Sarah, keen on making informed investment decisions, must weigh several factors before deciding to invest in Tesla.

Innovative Leadership and Vision:

Elon Musk's vision for Tesla is nothing short of revolutionary, and his leadership has been the driving force behind the company's continued success and innovation. Here's an analysis of Musk's vision and how it keeps Tesla at the forefront of technological advancements, along with some illustrative examples.

1. Accelerating the World's Transition to Sustainable Energy:
   - **Vision:** Musk's vision is centered on reducing the world's dependence on fossil fuels and promoting the use of renewable energy. This vision is not just about cars but

encompasses energy solutions for homes, businesses, and even entire power grids.
- **Example:** Tesla's Solar Roof and Powerwall products aim to enable homeowners to generate and store their own energy, reducing reliance on the grid and fossil fuels.

2. Innovation in Electric Vehicles (EVs):

- **Vision:** Musk envisions a future where electric vehicles are not just an alternative but the primary mode of transportation. He aims to produce EVs that outperform traditional combustion engine vehicles in terms of performance, safety, and affordability.
- **Example:** The Tesla Model 3. Designed to be a mass-market electric car, the Model 3 combines high performance with affordability, making EVs accessible to a broader audience.

3. Autonomous Driving:

- **Vision:** Musk is a strong advocate for autonomous driving technology. He believes self-driving cars will drastically reduce traffic accidents, increase productivity, and provide greater mobility to those unable to drive.
- **Example:** Tesla's Full Self-Driving (FSD) software. This advanced driver-assistance system, with features like Navigate on Autopilot and Smart Summon, is

continuously updated to move closer to fully autonomous driving capabilities.

4. Expansion into New Markets and Technologies:
- **Vision:** Musk is always looking ahead, seeking to expand Tesla's influence into new and innovative markets. This includes cars, trucks, sports cars, and even robotics.
- **Example:** The Tesla Semi and Cybertruck. Both products are designed to disrupt their respective markets with superior performance, sustainability, and futuristic designs.

5. Integration of AI and Robotics:
- **Vision:** Artificial intelligence and robotics play crucial roles in improving efficiency and quality of life. Musk aims to integrate these technologies into Tesla's products and operations.
- **Example:** The Tesla Bot (Optimus). Announced as a humanoid robot designed to perform repetitive or dangerous tasks, this project exemplifies Musk's commitment to advancing AI and robotics.

The Secret to Tesla's Stock Market Success

New Product Announcements

Anticipated new product launches, such as advancements in autonomous driving and energy storage solutions, could drive up Tesla's stock price.

1. Cybertruck:
   - **Description:** Tesla's futuristic all-electric pickup truck features a distinctive, angular design made from ultra-hard 30X cold-rolled stainless steel.
   - **Impact:** The Cybertruck is designed to compete with traditional pickup trucks, offering superior durability, performance, and features like adaptive air suspension and a range of up to 500 miles on a single charge.

2. Tesla Semi:
   - **Description:** An all-electric semi-truck designed to revolutionize the trucking industry with lower operational costs, enhanced safety features, and zero emissions.
   - **Impact:** The Tesla Semi aims to significantly reduce fuel costs and maintenance compared to traditional diesel trucks, which could attract logistics and freight companies.

Daluxe Inc.

3. Tesla Roadster:
   - **Description:** A high-performance sports car that promises to be the fastest production car ever made, with a top speed of over 250 mph.
   - **Impact:** The new Roadster is expected to showcase Tesla's technological prowess and attract high-end buyers looking for unparalleled speed and performance in an electric vehicle.

4. Full Self-Driving (FSD) Software:
   - **Description:** Tesla's advanced autonomous driving technology aims to enable fully autonomous driving capabilities through continuous software updates.
   - **Impact:** The FSD software could revolutionize how people drive, reducing accidents and increasing convenience. It could place Tesla at the forefront of autonomous vehicle technology if successfully implemented.

5. Solar Roof:
   - **Description:** A solar energy solution that integrates solar panels seamlessly into roof tiles, providing energy generation without compromising aesthetics.

- **Impact:** The Solar Roof aims to make sustainable energy more accessible and visually appealing.

6. Powerwall and Powerpack:
    - **Description:** Energy storage solutions designed for homes (Powerwall) and businesses/utility-scale installations (Powerpack), enabling efficient storage and use of solar energy.
    - **Impact:** These products can help consumers reduce reliance on the grid, lower energy costs, and provide backup power, enhancing Tesla's position in the renewable energy market.

7. Tesla Bot (Optimus):
    - **Description:** A humanoid robot is intended to assist in factories, homes, and other environments.
    - **Impact:** If successful, the Tesla Bot could revolutionize labor-intensive industries and introduce new efficiencies in both commercial and domestic settings.

Daluxe Inc.

8. RoboTaxi

- **Description:** Tesla's self-driving, all-electric taxi service offers a glimpse into the future of urban transportation, where hailing a ride doesn't require a driver. Powered by Tesla's Full Self-Driving (FSD) software, RoboTaxi promises a fully autonomous, convenient, and eco-friendly solution to modern transportation.
- **Impact:** RoboTaxi is poised to shake up the ride-hailing industry, replacing traditional taxis and rideshares with fully autonomous vehicles. Not only does it cut emissions, but it also slashes the cost of rides, as there's no driver to pay. It's the ultimate hands-free, eco-friendly way to get from point A to point B—sit back, relax, and let the car think.

9. RoboVan

- **Description:** Tesla's futuristic fully electric van is designed for personal and commercial use. It features spacious interiors, cutting-edge self-driving technology, and a sleek, minimalist design resembling something out of a sci-fi movie set.
- **Impact:** The RoboVan is set to revolutionize logistics, family road trips, and everything in between. Equipped with Tesla's Full Self-Driving (FSD) system, it's perfect for autonomous

deliveries while offering zero emissions. Whether hauling groceries or delivering packages, this van is the multitasking powerhouse of the future.

These new product announcements demonstrate Tesla's commitment to innovation and expanding its product line beyond electric vehicles. However, it's important to note that the successful market adoption of these products is not guaranteed, and there are potential challenges and risks, such as regulatory hurdles, competition, and technological limitations. Investing in Tesla could be a bet on these forward-looking technologies and their successful market adoption, but it's crucial to consider these factors when making investment decisions.

Financial Performance:

In the second quarter of 2024, Tesla's performance has shown improvement.

Quarter	Revenue (in billions)	Net Income (in billions)	Gross Margin (%)	Free Cash Flow (in billions)
Q1 2024	21.3	1.17	17.35	-2.53
Q2 2024	25.5	1.48	17.95	1.34

Revenue Growth: Despite supply chain challenges, Tesla's revenue has increased, a testament to its resilience and capacity to deliver vehicles and expand its energy business.

Daluxe Inc.

Net Income: Tesla's net income increased despite higher investments in future technologies, such as autonomous driving and production expansion.

Gross Margin: Gross margin has continued to increase, especially with Tesla's expansion of new vehicle lines and investment in technology development.

Free Cash Flow: Free cash flow has significantly increased and remains strong due to operational efficiencies despite Tesla's ongoing investments in new factories and technology.

Key Observations:

In the second quarter of 2024, Tesla demonstrated solid financial growth, especially in terms of revenue, net income, and gross margins. The company's profitability, solid free cash flow, and capability to manage growth and investment should provide reassurance to stakeholders. Tesla's primary focus is on establishing dominance in the electric vehicle and autonomous driving markets, which could result in significant returns in the future, despite current fluctuations in income and margins.

The Secret to Tesla's Stock Market Success

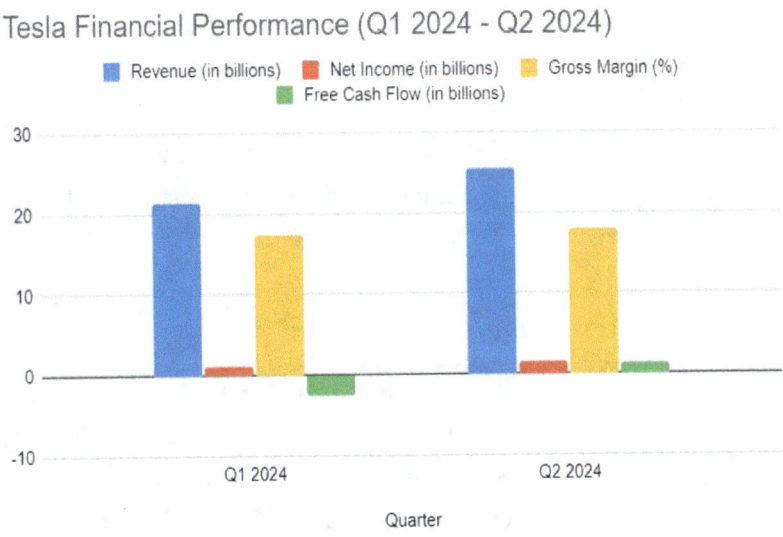

Stay Ahead: Check Tesla's Quarterly Reports

Please visit Tesla's official website for the most current and detailed breakdown of Tesla's financial performance. They regularly publish their quarterly reports, which provide comprehensive information. It's always a good idea to verify these numbers. You can find the latest data on revenue, net income, and other financial details in the investor relations section. This will give you an up-to-date look at the numbers.

Daluxe Inc.

Concerns about Tesla

1. Price Volatility:
   - Tesla's stock price is known for its volatility, which can be risky for investors seeking stability.

2. Operational Challenges:
   - **Production Bottlenecks:** Tesla has faced production and supply chain challenges, which could impact future performance.
   - **Quality Issues:** Recurring quality control issues and recalls could hurt Tesla's reputation and financials.

3. Market and Economic Factors:
   - **Economic Uncertainty:** Global economic conditions, including inflation and interest rate changes, can impact consumer spending on high-ticket items like cars.
   - **Competition:** Increasing competition from established automakers and new entrants in the EV market could erode Tesla's market share.

Investment Decision

Sarah should consider her investment horizon, risk tolerance, and belief in Tesla's prospects. While Tesla offers exciting growth potential, it's crucial to remain cautious of the high valuation and potential volatility. Careful analysis and a strategic approach will help Sarah make a well-informed decision.

Given the mixed factors, Tesla presents both opportunities and risks. It could be a good investment if Sarah tolerates volatility and believes in Tesla's long-term growth potential driven by innovation and market leadership.

Conclusion: The Investment Rollercoaster

Much like riding one of Elon Musk's Hyperloops, investing in Tesla is a journey filled with highs, lows, and rapid changes. The key takeaway from this case study is that a thorough understanding of internal, external, and seasonal factors is crucial for making well-informed investment decisions in Tesla.

Daluxe Inc.

Chapter 8: The Role of Stagflation in Tesla's Stock Movements

Stagflation combines high inflation, slow growth, and rising unemployment. It's like the economy is in reverse while prices keep climbing. Adding Tesla's stock makes things more interesting.

Stagflation complicates the usual economic indicators, causing Tesla's stock to be as unpredictable as one of Elon Musk's tweets. High inflation increases the cost of building Teslas, while slow growth and job losses result in fewer buyers for electric vehicles. In this chapter, we will examine how this unusual economic situation affects Tesla's stock and why stagflation could disrupt Tesla's steady performance.

Analyzing Economic Signals and Tesla's Stock Performance

While Tesla is known for its innovation, it is still influenced by traditional economic factors that impact its stock value. Economic indicators can be likened to a doctor's stethoscope, providing essential insights into the economy's overall health. And just like you wouldn't ignore your doctor's advice (hopefully), you should consider how these indicators influence Tesla's market moves. Let's break it down in plain, Tesla-friendly terms.

GDP: The Economy's Report Card

Gross Domestic Product (GDP) is the economy's saying, "Here's how much stuff we made this year." When GDP is up, people spend, invest, and, crucially, buy more Teslas. A growing economy is like rocket fuel for companies—there's more money flowing around, and that's excellent news for Tesla, especially since their cars aren't exactly in the budget category. But when GDP takes a nosedive, the economy slows, and people start tightening their belts. Suddenly, that shiny new Tesla doesn't seem as affordable, and stock prices can reflect that belt-tightening.

Interest Rates: The Cost of Money

Interest rates are like the price tag on borrowing money, and they significantly impact whether or not someone will pull the trigger on financing a Tesla. When interest rates increase, borrowing money to buy a new car becomes pricier. That means fewer people are signing up for Tesla's latest model—and that can take the wind out of Tesla's stock price sails. On the flip side, when interest rates are low, it's a green light for consumers to borrow. Financing is cheaper, and more people are likely to jump on the EV bandwagon, boosting sales and, you guessed it, stock prices.

Unemployment Rate: The Workforce Wallet

The unemployment rate tells us how many people are out of work, and it's more important than just knowing who's skipping the morning commute. High unemployment means fewer people with steady paychecks, which translates to less money spent on things like high-end electric cars. No matter how eco-friendly or fast Tesla's cars are, they're still a luxury for most people. When jobs are scarce, so are Tesla buyers. Conversely, when unemployment is low, people are gainfully employed and have more cash to spend. That's great news for Tesla's sales figures—and even better for its stock price.

Inflation: The Sneaky Price Creep

Ah, inflation—the slow, sneaky rise in prices that makes your money worth a little less every year. While inflation can affect everyone, it's tricky for companies like Tesla. If inflation drives up the cost of raw materials—like the batteries, chips, and metals that go into every Tesla—those increased costs can either eat into profits or force Tesla to raise its prices. Neither option is great for the stock price. On the flip side, if inflation remains under control, Tesla can keep its production costs in check, and that's a win for investors.

Consumer Confidence: The Market Mood Ring

Consumer confidence is like a national mood ring—it measures people's optimism about their financial future. When confidence is high, people are likely to make big purchases, like a Tesla Model S. But when the mood shifts toward uncertainty, people tend to hold off on luxury buys. If consumers don't feel confident about their economic prospects, it can result in fewer sales and a dip in Tesla's stock price.

The Secret to Tesla's Stock Market Success

While Tesla is a cutting-edge tech giant, its stock price still responds to the economy's ebb and flow. When economic indicators are flashing green—like solid GDP growth, low interest rates, low unemployment, and high consumer confidence—Tesla's stock tends to soar. However, Tesla's stock can hit a speed bump when the economy falters. Understanding these indicators can help you anticipate how external factors might impact Tesla's performance, so you're ready to ride the stock market waves like a pro.

What is a Recession? An Explanation of Economic Downturns

A **recession** is a period of economic decline marked by a significant drop in economic activity. It's typically recognized when a country's Gross Domestic Product (GDP) contracts for two consecutive quarters. Still, it can also involve other key indicators such as rising unemployment, reduced consumer spending, and declining industrial production.

During a recession, businesses may reduce production, leading to job losses and reduced incomes. Consumers tend to spend less, which further slows down the economy. Companies often face lower profits, and stock markets can decline as investors lose confidence in future growth.

Recessions are part of the natural economic cycle and can be triggered by factors such as high inflation, rising interest rates, supply chain disruptions, or financial crises. While recessions can be challenging, they are usually followed by a recovery phase where economic activity reoccurs. Governments and central banks often step in with policies, like lowering interest rates or increasing public spending, to help stimulate the economy and mitigate the impact of a recession.

How to Predict a Recession Using Economic Indicators

Predicting a recession using economic indicators involves analyzing key signs that signal an economic slowdown. While no single indicator guarantees a recession, specific trends and patterns can offer strong warnings.

Gross Domestic Product (GDP)

GDP measures a country's total output of goods and services. A decline in GDP for two consecutive quarters is a classic recession signal. Monitoring GDP growth trends can help detect when the economy is contracting.

Unemployment Rate

A rising unemployment rate is often one of the earliest signs of economic trouble. As businesses struggle, they reduce their workforce, leading to higher unemployment. Consistent increases in unemployment rates signal a weakening economy and potential recession.

Consumer Confidence

Consumer confidence measures people's optimism about the economy and their financial future. A significant drop in consumer confidence indicates that people are less likely to spend, which can slow economic growth and trigger a recession.

Inflation and Interest Rates

High inflation paired with rising interest rates can indicate an economy overheating. Central banks often raise interest rates to combat inflation, but higher rates make borrowing more expensive, which can reduce spending and investment, potentially leading to a recession.

Daluxe Inc.

Manufacturing Activity

A drop in manufacturing output can signal that demand is weakening. Manufacturing data, such as the Purchasing Managers' Index (PMI), can show whether production is slowing, often a sign of economic contraction.

Federal Reserve Economic Data (FRED)

FRED, managed by the Federal Reserve Bank of St. Louis, offers various financial statistics, charts, and graphs, from unemployment rates to inflation trends. It's a valuable resource for economists, investors, and anyone interested in economic trends, and it's free to use!

To get the Consumer Confidence Index, visit FRED, type "Consumer Confidence Index" into the search bar, click on the result, and voila—you're suddenly an economic data guru!

In short, by closely monitoring these indicators—GDP, unemployment, consumer confidence, inflation, the yield curve, the stock market, and manufacturing activity—economists and investors can better understand whether a recession may be approaching. While predicting a recession isn't foolproof, these signals offer valuable insights into the economy's health.

Recession vs. Stagflation: Economic Downturn vs. High Inflation and Unemployment

The difference between **recession** and **stagflation** is like comparing a cold to the flu—neither is fun, but one has a particularly nasty twist.

Recession

A recession is when the economy decides to take a nap. You'll notice GDP shrinking, unemployment rising, and people generally tightening their belts because spending and investment have slowed down. It's a time when businesses make less money, jobs get cut, and the stock market throws a tantrum. Think of it as the economy hitting the brakes for a while.

Stagflation

Stagflation, on the other hand, could be more sneakier and a lot more confusing. It's like the economy is struggling with a high fever *and* refusing to get out of bed, presenting a complex challenge. Stagflation is when you get the worst of both worlds: the economy isn't growing (hence the "stag" part), but inflation is rising (the "inflation" part). So, prices keep climbing, but people need to make more money to keep up, and unemployment might be rising too. It's like trying to pedal a bike uphill while the brakes are stuck and the tires are flat.

The Nasty Twist

In a recession, prices stay stable or fall because people aren't spending as much. But with stagflation, prices rise despite the economic slowdown, meaning everything gets more expensive while jobs and wages are in the dumps. It's like the economy is misbehaving and charging you extra for it!

In short, a recession is a slowdown, while stagflation is a frustrating combo of rising prices and no growth. Neither is pleasant, but overcoming stagflation requires particular resilience and determination, making it challenging to shake off.

The Impact of Stagflation on Tesla's Stock Performance

Stagflation is a challenging combination of rising inflation and stagnant economic growth, similar to a vehicle trapped in traffic with increasing fuel and no escape route. Consider navigating this complex scenario, which illustrates how even a pioneering company such as Tesla can encounter obstacles on the stock market journey.

Understanding Stagflation: A Crucial Concept for Investors

In most cases, inflation and growth tend to move together. Inflation increases when the economy performs well, as does employment and consumer spending. Stagflation is an economic situation in which inflation is rising, but the economy is not growing, and unemployment is rising.

In stagflation, something has gone wrong in the financial crisis. This is terrible news for most businesses. Stagflation creates uncertainty. It's not just about whether prices are increasing or decreasing; it's about the system slowing down while costs spin out of control. Companies like Tesla, which depend on growth, consumer spending, and advanced production processes, are typically at risk.

Understanding Economic Indicators in the Context of Stagflation

Economic indicators are like the dashboard of a car—they provide necessary signals about the economy's health. When everything runs smoothly, indicators such as GDP, inflation, and unemployment give us a clear picture of growth, stability, and spending power. But when stagflation occurs, these indicators send mixed signals, much like warning lights going off simultaneously.

GDP (Gross Domestic Product)

Usually, GDP measures the total value of goods and services produced in a country, and when it's growing, the economy is healthy. However, during stagflation, GDP growth slows or even contracts, meaning the economy is barely moving, if at all. Even though inflation is rising (which usually signals growth), GDP lags, creating the "stagnant" part of stagflation. This contradiction between rising prices and weak growth makes stagflation particularly tricky for businesses like Tesla, as they face higher costs but less overall economic activity.

Inflation

Inflation is the rate at which prices for goods and services rise. In a normal economy, moderate inflation is expected and even desired, signaling demand. But during stagflation, inflation keeps climbing despite the weak economy. This makes everything more expensive—from groceries to raw materials like steel and lithium. For companies like Tesla, inflation pushes production costs higher, squeezing profit margins. Consumers also face higher prices for everyday items, which can make luxury purchases like electric vehicles less affordable.

Unemployment

In a healthy economy, unemployment stays low because businesses are expanding and hiring. However, in stagflation, unemployment often rises while inflation continues. This combination is fierce: more people are out of work, but the cost of living is increasing. For companies like Tesla, this means fewer consumers with the financial ability to buy expensive electric vehicles. As unemployment rises, consumer confidence drops and demand for luxury goods like Teslas falls.

How These Indicators Combine in Stagflation

Rising inflation might signify a strong economy with increasing demand in normal economic conditions. But in stagflation, inflation runs wild while GDP stagnates and unemployment rises. This means that prices are increasing for everything— including the cost of producing cars and energy solutions—while fewer people can afford to buy. It creates a vicious cycle where businesses struggle with higher costs, and consumers cut back on spending.

For Tesla, stagflation is a looming threat: production becomes more expensive, but fewer people are in a position to buy their cars. And as the economy stalls, investors might lose confidence, affecting Tesla's stock performance.

Timing Tesla Stock During Stagflation

So, how do you, as an investor, navigate Tesla's stock during stagflation? Timing is when Tesla's production costs rise and demand falls, and Tesla's stock might go through a rough patch. However, savvy investors can capitalize on these downturns. Historically, economic slumps have provided opportunities to buy quality stocks at lower prices.

The trick is to monitor macroeconomic indicators—like inflation rates, unemployment, and consumer spending trends. If these signals show Tesla's stagflation, it might be a warning that Tesla's stock is headed for turbulence. But as any seasoned investor will tell you, downturns can also be a time for companies at a discount. If you believe in Tesla's long-term innovation and ability to ride out economic storms, buying during a stagflation-induced dip could pay off when the economy bounces back.

Chapter 9: Algo Trading and Tesla Stock: Understanding High-Frequency Movements

Predictive Models and Tools

Alright, fellow adventurers in the wild world of Tesla stock, get ready to harness the power of predictive models and tools—your new best friends in this exhilarating roller coaster. These models are not just crystal balls, they're packed with data, algorithms, and a dash of mathematical magic, empowering you to make informed decisions. And no, you don't need to wave a wand to use them, though it might make the process more fun.

So, what exactly are predictive models? They're sophisticated algorithms designed to analyze historical data and identify patterns that can forecast future performance. Imagine Sherlock Holmes, but he's predicting stock movements instead of solving crimes.

One popular tool in our predictive arsenal is Time Series Analysis. This method involves collecting data points at regular intervals and analyzing them to identify trends, cycles, and seasonal variations. Think of it as plotting Tesla's stock prices on a timeline and then using statistical techniques to predict where they'll go next. It's like reading tea leaves but with more spreadsheets and fewer superstitions.

Time Series Analysis

Time series analysis is used in statistics to analyze time-ordered data points. By observing how values change over time, one can make predictions about future trends. In the context of stock market data, such as Tesla's stock prices, time series analysis can help forecast future stock movements based on historical patterns.

Example of Time Series Analysis on Tesla Stock

The Secret to Tesla's Stock Market Success

Dataset

For this example, let's consider Tesla's stock price data collected weekly from 2013 to 2023.

Steps in Time Series Analysis:

1. **Trend Analysis:** Identify any long-term trends in the data. One might observe significant growth trends for Tesla, especially during periods surrounding major company milestones like product launches or earnings announcements.
2. **Seasonality Analysis:** Look for patterns that repeat at regular intervals. This might be harder to discern for stocks but could relate to quarterly financial reports or yearly industry events.
3. **Cyclical Effects:** Unlike seasonality, cyclical effects are not of fixed periods. Economic cycles or broader automotive industry trends might affect Tesla's stock.

Analysis of Tesla Stock

From 2013 to 2023, Tesla's stock showed remarkable growth, especially from mid-2020 onwards. This period includes significant product announcements and expansions, such as constructing new Gigafactories and launching new vehicle models.

1. **Trend:** The long-term trend shows upward solid growth.
2. **Seasonal Variations:** While less pronounced, Tesla stock might exhibit volatility around quarterly earnings reports.
3. **Cyclical Influence:** Economic factors such as interest rates or automotive sector performance can influence stock prices cyclically.

Using the Time Series Analysis model on this data, one could forecast that, barring unforeseen circumstances, Tesla's stock might continue its upward trajectory in the long term, influenced by its innovation cycle and market expansion plans.

The Secret to Tesla's Stock Market Success

Source: TradingView

Over the past decade, Tesla's stock chart has unfolded like an epic saga, punctuated by crucial turning points. Starting from a modest base of around $1 in 2010, the stock has defied gravity, climbing to over $400 by 2021. This phenomenal rise is a tale of electrifying cars and a narrative woven with innovation, market expansion, and a touch of audacity.

Act I: The Early Struggles (2010-2013)

Tesla's stock performance was a testament to the company's resilience, resembling an underdog story. Despite the market being dominated by established automotive giants, the stock price meandered between $1 and $20, reflecting the skepticism of investors yet to be convinced by the electric car revolution. This early struggle, however, was a precursor to the company's eventual breakthrough, inspiring all who witnessed it.

Act II: The Breakthrough (2013-2016)

The narrative took a dramatic turn as Tesla began delivering on its promises. Investors started to notice, and the stock surged from around $20 to nearly $200. This period marked Tesla's transition from a speculative investment to a proven solid company.

Act III: The Rocket Ship (2016-2021)

This period was nothing short of a blockbuster if the previous acts were compelling. With the introduction of the Model 3, which aimed at the mass market, Tesla's stock performance mimicked a rocket ship. It shot up with breathtaking speed, propelled by soaring revenues, production milestones, and a charismatic CEO who seemed to thrive on breaking norms. In 2020, Tesla's stock had crossed the $400 mark.

Forecasting the Future: The Sequel to Watch

The Secret to Tesla's Stock Market Success

Using time series analysis on this data, one might forecast that, barring unforeseen plot twists (like a surprise villain or an unexpected market crash), Tesla's stock could continue its upward trajectory in the long term. The potential for this trajectory is a crucial point of interest for investors and analysts alike, instilling a sense of optimism about the company's future.

Innovation Cycle

Tesla's commitment to innovation is akin to a never-ending series of sequels, each more exciting than the last. This relentless innovation cycle will likely keep investor interest and stock prices buoyant.

Market Expansion Plans

Tesla's ambitions to expand its market reach are as grand as any blockbuster's special effects budget. With new gigafactories sprouting across continents and the foray into new markets such as India and Southeast Asia, Tesla is set on a path of global dominance. This geographic diversification reduces risk and opens new revenue streams, supporting long-term stock price growth.

Daluxe Inc.

Economic Conditions and Market Sentiment

The broader economic conditions and market sentiment will play crucial roles in Tesla's stock performance. While the company has shown resilience, it is not entirely immune to macroeconomic factors such as interest rates, inflation, and geopolitical events. However, the bullish sentiment towards green technologies and sustainable investments provides a favorable backdrop for Tesla.

Conclusion: The Final Curtain Call?

In conclusion, Tesla's stock story is one of relentless innovation, strategic market expansion, and a bit of theatrical flair. While past performance does not always indicate future results, the trends suggest that Tesla's stock might continue to script an upward trajectory. So, grab your popcorn and hold onto your seats; the Tesla stock saga is far from over, and the next act promises to be as thrilling as the last.

Disclaimer: A Word to the Wise

Before you dash off to invest your life savings in Tesla, based on this captivating analysis, let's hit the pause button and sprinkle in a dash of reality and humor. This scintillating piece of financial theater is purely for entertainment and intellectual amusement. It's not, I repeat, **not** legal or financial advice.

Think of this analysis as the movie trailer before the main feature – exciting and intriguing, but not the whole story. The stock market is a fickle beast, prone to unexpected twists and turns that even the best predictors can't foresee. So, while we've had some fun forecasting Tesla's future, remember that investing requires more than just a hearty laugh and a hopeful heart.

Take this analysis with a grain of salt, a dash of skepticism, and perhaps a pinch of popcorn. It's important to consult your financial advisor (the real-life one, not the one in your head) before making investment decisions. After all, it's your hard-earned money on the line, and we want to ensure it stays happy and healthy, just like you. This will make you feel responsible and informed about your investment decisions.

Machine Learning

Machine learning is like a crystal ball for data in finance—it analyzes past trends and predicts what's coming next. I know what you're thinking: "Are we building robots to trade stocks?" Not quite, but close! Machine learning involves training algorithms on vast data to learn patterns and make predictions.

Daluxe Inc.

It's like teaching your dog to fetch, but instead of sticks, it's fetching profitable insights. Algorithms such as regression models, neural networks, and decision trees become your companions, sniffing out trends and potential pitfalls.

One particularly flashy tool in the machine learning toolbox is the Neural Network. Inspired by the human brain (minus the existential dread), neural networks are designed to recognize patterns in complex datasets. They're especially good at handling non-linear relationships—perfect for a stock like Tesla that can be as predictable as a cat on catnip. With neural networks, you're essentially unleashing a mini-brain to analyze the chaotic dance of stock prices and predict their next move.

But wait, there's more! Let's remember the trusty Monte Carlo Simulation. Picture it running thousands of "what if" scenarios to see how Tesla's stock might react to various events, like a new product launch or Elon Musk tweeting about Dogecoin. The results give you a probability distribution of potential outcomes, helping you navigate the stormy seas of stock investing.

Predictive models and tools are invaluable in forecasting Tesla's stock performance cycles. They transform the unpredictable into the somewhat foreseeable, giving you a fighting chance in the fast-paced world of stock investing. So, embrace these tools, stay informed, and may your investments be ever in your favor. And remember, even the best models are just that—models. The real world has a funny way of surprising us all, so always be cautious and mindful in your investment decisions.

Machine Learning and Timing Tesla's Stock

One of the most prominent players in the machine learning game is BlackRock, the world's largest asset manager, managing a mind-blowing $10 trillion in assets. Founded in 1988, BlackRock has since become a giant in the financial world, and like any giant, it has its secret weapon: an AI platform called Aladdin. Aladdin stands for Asset, Liability, Debt, and Derivative Investment Network. This AI powerhouse crunches billions of data points daily, acting like the ultimate financial wizard. It's like having an army of analysts and economists working around the clock—except they're faster, more accurate, and don't need coffee breaks.

But Aladdin isn't just about numbers. It's a multitasker that reads market sentiment, analyzes financial reports, and tracks global news events to predict how they'll impact stocks, bonds, and other assets.

The real magic behind Aladdin is algorithms. Algorithms, or "algos" for short, are like the Formula 1 cars of the financial world. They are pre-programmed sets of rules that automatically execute trades without human intervention. This automatic nature allows them to react faster than humans and reduces the potential for human error. Aladdin, originally BlackRock's secret sauce, is now used by major players worldwide, including pension funds, banks, and even entire countries like Norway and Saudi Arabia.

Going up against algorithms in the stock market can feel like racing a bicycle against a Ferrari. These trading robots work 24/7, processing data and making moves without hesitation. But here's the good news: you can still win, especially if you play it smart.

Algorithms are great for quick, short-term trades. You, on the other hand, can focus on long-term investments and stick to your game plan. With the right data tools at your fingertips, you can also access market insights. The key is to avoid emotional trading and trust your data—remember, algorithms don't have feelings, but we do.

AI Trading Platforms for Everyday Investors

You don't need a supercomputer to get in on the action. For traders in the US and Canada seeking AI-based trading insights, several platforms provide tools that utilize machine learning to assist in making wiser investment decisions. The following are some popular options:

The Secret to Tesla's Stock Market Success

Trade Ideas

This platform is highly regarded in the US and Canada. It uses AI-driven trading to generate real-time stock recommendations and trade ideas. Their AI engine, Holly, evaluates millions of trading strategies every day and identifies the ones with the highest potential. It's great for traders who want to use AI to identify patterns and trends in real-time.

- Key Feature: Pre-market and real-time alerts.
- Great for Day traders and swing traders.

Kavout

Using its Kai score, Kavout offers an AI-driven platform that provides stock ratings and trade signals. The platform analyzes large datasets, including financials, market sentiment, and news reports, to give investors stock insights and signals. It's available in both the US and Canada.

- Key Feature: Kai Score ranks stocks based on machine learning models.
- Great for: Long-term investors looking for AI-enhanced stock ratings.

QuantConnect

This is more of a quantitative trading platform but offers powerful tools for building AI-based trading strategies. It's ideal for advanced traders who want to develop and backtest their trading algorithms. It's available in both the US and Canada.

- Key Feature: Allows users to build and backtest custom algorithms.
- Great for Algorithmic traders and quantitative investors.

Tickeron

Tickeron offers AI-driven insights for stocks and cryptocurrencies. The platform has tools like Pattern Search Engine and AI Trend Forecasts that use machine learning to spot stock patterns and make predictive analytics available to retail investors in the US and Canada.

- Key Feature: Predictive pattern recognition.
- Great for Both beginner and advanced traders.

ThinkorSwim by TD Ameritrade

A robust trading platform with advanced charting tools, ThinkorSwim offers AI-powered analysis features for technical

The Secret to Tesla's Stock Market Success

traders. While it doesn't have an AI engine like Trade Ideas' Holly, it does have features that use predictive analytics and pattern recognition to help traders make informed decisions. It's available in both the US and Canada.

- Key Feature: AI-enhanced technical analysis tools.
- Great for Options traders, stock traders, and technical analysis enthusiasts.

These platforms provide various AI-powered tools to help you gain an advantage in the market, whether you are a casual investor or a more advanced trader. While AI can provide valuable insights, combining its advice with your own research is always wise.

Daluxe Inc.

Chapter 10: The Future of Tesla Stock: Beyond Cars

Tesla's future is not just about revolutionizing the automotive industry but about transforming entire sectors with cutting-edge energy, AI, and robotics technology. So, get ready because the road involves more than zero-emission vehicles; it's filled with renewable energy, autonomous taxis, and maybe even a robot that makes your morning coffee.

Tesla Energy: Powering More Than Cars

Daluxe Inc.

When most people think of Tesla, they think of sleek electric cars zipping silently down the highway. But beneath the hood of Tesla's high-tech automotive image lies something far more ambitious: Tesla Energy. This isn't just about driving; it's about powering the world—which might be Tesla's most exciting growth engine. While Elon Musk is known for shaking up the auto industry, Tesla Energy could turn him into the energy tycoon of the 21st century, minus the cowboy hat and oil rigs.

Solar Roofs and the Home of Tomorrow

Tesla's Solar Roof isn't just a bunch of solar panels slapped on your house. No, these solar tiles look sleek and blend in with modern architecture. In the future, Tesla envisions a world where your home is a fully autonomous, solar-powered hub. Imagine the house of tomorrow, where every rooftop is soaking up the sun like a giant, high-tech sponge, turning sunlight into pure, clean energy. And when the sun's down, Tesla's Powerwall stores that energy, powering your Netflix binge session or your late-night snack runs to the fridge.

As solar energy becomes cheaper and more efficient, we will likely see a surge in the number of homeowners and businesses switching to Tesla's solar solutions. It's not just about reducing electricity bills but also achieving energy independence. In the future, energy grids could become more decentralized, with

Tesla Energy leading the charge, allowing homes to produce and store their electricity.

Tesla Powerwall and Powerpack: Battery-Powered Future

Batteries might not be as glamorous as Tesla's Cybertruck, but they're equally crucial to the company's future. Tesla's Powerwall for homes and Powerpack for commercial use offer energy storage solutions critical for the widespread adoption of renewable energy. Why? Because the sun doesn't always shine, and the wind doesn't always blow—but your lights still need to work when you flip the switch.

In the future, as renewable energy sources like wind and solar become the norm, the demand for battery storage will skyrocket. Tesla is positioning itself to dominate this space. Think of Powerwall as the Siri of home energy—it works behind the scenes, ensuring your home stays powered up even when the grid goes down. Powerpack, meanwhile, is like its beefier cousin, handling the needs of factories, businesses, and even entire cities.

Tesla's battery products will become even more essential in a world shifting towards renewable energy. The days of relying on traditional power plants could be numbered. Tesla's energy storage solutions will likely play a significant role in shaping a future where renewable energy isn't just a dream but the new normal.

Tesla Energy's Role in the Grid of the Future

The future of energy is decentralized, and Tesla Energy is building the tools to make that possible. Instead of relying on giant, centralized power plants, future energy grids will be more intelligent, resilient, and, most importantly, decentralized. Tesla's vision is a world where homes, businesses, and even cars are all energy producers, contributing to a vast, interconnected web of power.

Tesla's energy products will likely play a vital role in the future. Homes equipped with Solar Roofs and Powerwalls can generate and store electricity, while Powerpacks can stabilize the grid during peak demand. When millions of Tesla vehicles are plugged into charging stations, they could become mobile energy storage units, feeding power back into the grid during critical moments. It's a world where energy is shared, stored, and managed efficiently—and Tesla is at the heart of it all.

Environmental Impact and Tesla's Global Role

Beyond the financial upside, Tesla Energy's success has massive environmental implications. As global demand for clean energy grows, Tesla's products will help reduce reliance on fossil fuels and shrink carbon footprints worldwide. And with global initiatives pushing for greener energy policies, Tesla is uniquely positioned to benefit from regulatory shifts towards sustainability.

The Future is Bright, and It's Solar-Powered

In conclusion, Tesla's energy business could one day rival its automotive division. With solar, storage, and a growing global footprint, Tesla is poised to dominate the renewable energy market. The future isn't just cars driving in the sunshine—it's about entire cities running on Tesla's energy solutions. For investors, this means that Tesla's stock isn't just about electric vehicles; it's about powering the future in ways we're only beginning to understand.

Tesla as an AI-Driven Tech Company

Tesla's true secret weapon is Artificial Intelligence. It's not just a feature of the cars; it's the core of the company's future and the key to unlocking new industries and endless opportunities.

Daluxe Inc.

AI-Powered Cars: The Not-So-Distant Present

Tesla's Full Self-Driving (FSD) system is an advanced AI that constantly learns and improves. As more Tesla cars hit the road, their AI gets smarter. This technology could be used beyond driving cars, managing urban traffic systems, or creating intelligent cities where everything moves in perfect harmony. In essence, the future is about AI as the operating system of the entire transportation network.

AI in Energy: Smart Grids and Beyond

Let's delve into Tesla's energy business. While solar panels and Powerwalls are great, AI's role in optimizing energy use is the real game-changer. Tesla's AI manages energy grids, predicts energy needs, and optimizes real-time storage to create intelligent energy systems that handle renewable energy sources like solar and wind. It can revolutionize energy management for entire cities, ensuring no watt goes to waste.

Optimus: AI-Powered Robots

Tesla's humanoid robot, Optimus, represents the potential of AI-driven robotics outside of cars. With Tesla's AI expertise, Optimus could revolutionize industries like manufacturing, logistics, and healthcare, creating an AI-powered workforce that never tires, reduces costs, and pushes Tesla's stock to new heights.

AI as Tesla's DNA: The Google or Apple of Tomorrow

Tesla's future is less about selling electric cars and more about becoming an AI-driven tech giant. Think of Tesla in 10 years—do you see a car company or company leading in AI, robotics, energy management, and maybe even healthcare? Tesla is already leveraging data in ways that most traditional automakers can't even fathom. Its AI-driven systems don't just collect data; they process it, learn from it, and improve themselves continuously. Tesla's data advantage could turn into an AI ecosystem that is not limited to vehicles but expands into every facet of modern life—from managing cities to automating industries and improving healthcare outcomes.

The Long-Term Growth Potential: AI Everywhere

Tesla's future lies in leveraging AI beyond the car industry. Tesla isn't just building electric vehicles—it's building a future where artificial intelligence shapes every corner of our lives. From optimizing energy grids, running autonomous taxis, and creating robot-powered factories, Tesla is poised to become a tech giant whose influence extends beyond roads and highways.

This AI-first approach could create new revenue streams, as Tesla's AI evolves and its applications are licensed to other industries. From autonomous taxis to AI-powered robots, Tesla's future is driven by AI.

RoboTaxi and Tesla's Growth: The Self-Driving Revolution

Tesla's RoboTaxi is shaping up to be a game-changer, not just in transportation but also in Tesla's overall growth strategy. Think of it as the Uber of the future—except there's no driver, no awkward conversations about the weather, and no tipping required.

New Revenue Streams

RoboTaxi opens up an entirely new revenue stream for Tesla. Instead of selling cars, Tesla is entering the ride-hailing business—one of the most lucrative sectors. With autonomous vehicles, Tesla eliminates the need for drivers, meaning Tesla keeps more of the fare. It's like running a fleet of taxis that never need a lunch break or vacation.

The Secret to Tesla's Stock Market Success

Fleet Potential

Tesla plans to launch a RoboTaxis network, where owners can add their cars to the fleet and earn money while not using them. Imagine your vehicle paying for itself while you're at work or sleeping! This model doesn't just sell cars—it makes them income-generating assets, which is bound to attract even more buyers to the Tesla brand.

Boost to Autonomy & AI Tech

RoboTaxi puts Tesla's Full Self-Driving (FSD) technology at the forefront. Every RoboTaxi on the road provides real-time data to improve Tesla's AI, further solidifying Tesla's leadership in autonomous driving tech.

Market Domination

RoboTaxi could reshape urban transportation, giving Tesla a foothold in a trillion-dollar market. Traditional ride-hailing services like Uber and Lyft must rethink their strategies while Tesla cruises ahead with fully autonomous, eco-friendly, and low-cost rides.

Stock Market Buzz

Let's remember the impact on Tesla's stock. The very mention of RoboTaxi gets investors excited. The idea of Tesla dominating the autonomous ride-hailing market sends the stock price buzzing with anticipation, contributing to Tesla's valuation and growth.

Optimus Robot: From Manufacturing to Healthcare

Tesla's Optimus Robot might sound like something straight out of a sci-fi blockbuster, but the reality is that this humanoid robot could have a far-reaching impact across industries. Optimus is currently strutting its stuff on Tesla's factory floors, but its future potential could make even the most futuristic predictions seem conservative.

Whether it's assembling car parts, delivering packages, or even caring for older people, Optimus is gearing up to take over various tasks that make it the multitool of the robotic world.

Manufacturing: A Robotic Workforce Revolution

Optimus is being developed to help with mundane and repetitive tasks at Tesla's Gigafactories. Think of it as the ultimate worker who doesn't need breaks never gets tired, and has absolutely no complaints about overtime. Optimus will revolutionize the factory floor, turning what used to require human labor into an entirely automated process. Tesla could deploy these robots in its factories and sell them to other manufacturing companies, making factories worldwide more efficient and, quite frankly, robot-run.

But here's where things get interesting: Optimus could lower Tesla's production costs while improving output, making their cars and possibly other products more affordable.

Logistics: Deliveries without Human Hands

Optimus could be walking down your street, delivering packages, or moving goods in warehouses with a precision that no human could match. Optimus could change the game in the logistics industry, where speed and efficiency are everything. Gone are the days of late deliveries and tired drivers—Optimus is the 24/7, rain-or-shine, never-needs-to-pee solution that logistics companies dream of.

Moving into this market would open up yet another revenue stream for Tesla. They wouldn't just be selling cars and energy products; they'd be selling robots that could deliver your new Tesla right to your doorstep! The logistics sector is already huge, but with Optimus, Tesla could help it leap into the future.

Healthcare: Optimus, the Robo-Nurse

Optimus could have a future in healthcare. Imagine Optimus being deployed in hospitals, nursing homes, and rehabilitation centers. Instead of overworked healthcare workers, we could see fleets of Optimus robots assisting patients with mobility, helping doctors with equipment, and even providing companionship to the elderly.

The healthcare industry faces labor shortages, particularly in caring for aging populations. Optimus could help bridge this gap by providing affordable, consistent, and tireless care to those who need it most. This would revolutionize healthcare and dramatically increase Tesla's market reach. Optimus could become a key player in a trillion-dollar industry, boosting Tesla's stock in ways the automotive sector could never achieve.

Optimus in Retail and Beyond

Optimus could easily be adapted for use in retail environments, handling tasks such as stocking, cleaning, and customer service.

The Secret to Tesla's Stock Market Success

Imagine walking into a store where Optimus greets you, helps you find what you're looking for, and checks you out at the register. This would save retailers on labor costs and provide consumers with an efficient and next-level shopping experience.

Optimus has the potential to revolutionize almost every industry. It's like the Swiss Army knife of robots, and each new application Tesla finds for it creates a new revenue stream that could propel the stock to new heights. This could mean massive growth potential for Tesla's stock beyond cars and energy. Each new market opens up a new growth trajectory, ensuring Tesla's dominance in more than just transportation.

Robotaxi: A Game-Changer for Revenue

Tesla's Robotaxi initiative represents the company's ambitious endeavor to establish dominance in the ride-hailing sector through driverless operations. Envision a scenario where fleets of autonomous Teslas seamlessly cater to transportation needs round-the-clock, potentially serving millions. This vision is not confined to the realm of science fiction; rather, Tesla stands on the brink of actualizing these self-driving fleets in the near future.

Robotaxi has the potential to position Tesla as a major player akin to Uber or Lyft, minus the reliance on human drivers.

Notably, Tesla stands to retain the entirety of the generated revenue, unburdened by driver commissions or associated logistical considerations. This translates to a scenario of pure profitability.

Tesla's AI capabilities, especially in autonomous driving and machine learning, are already far ahead of many competitors. As these technologies advance, Tesla is positioning itself as a car and tech company.

The Real Value: A Tech Conglomerate in the Making

At its core, Tesla isn't just selling cars—it's building an ecosystem of sustainable energy, AI, and automation. When you think of Tesla as an energy company, a ride-hailing service, a robotics leader, and an AI powerhouse, you realize its current valuation is just the tip of the iceberg.

In the future, Tesla's revenue won't be tied to the number of cars it sells. It'll come from solar power generation, energy storage, autonomous transportation, and AI-driven products and services. So, while some analysts might say Tesla's current stock price is overvalued, they're probably stuck thinking of it as a traditional car company.

The Secret to Tesla's Stock Market Success

The reality? Tesla is much, much more. It's a tech conglomerate in the making, with its fingers in some of the most lucrative pies of the future economy. Tesla's revenue will not only come from cars but also from solar panels, energy grids, autonomous fleets, robots, AI software, and more. So, if you're only looking at today's Tesla, it's time to look again—because the Tesla of tomorrow is about to redefine what it means to be a tech company in the 21st century.

References

IMF. (2024). *World Economic Outlook Update, January 2024: Moderating inflation and steady growth open path to soft landing*. (2024, January 30). IMF. https://www.imf.org/en/Publications/WEO/Issues/2024/01/30/world-economic-outlook-update-january-2024

BEA. (2024). *Gross domestic Product, first quarter 2024 (Advance Estimate) | U.S. Bureau of Economic Analysis (BEA)*. (n.d.). https://www.bea.gov/news/2024/gross-domestic-product-first-quarter-2024-advance-estimate

Neufeld, D. (2024, February 12). *Mapped: GDP Growth Forecasts by Country in 2024*. Visual Capitalist. https://www.visualcapitalist.com/gdp-growth-forecasts-by-country-in-2024/

University of Michigan: Consumer sentiment. (2024, September 27). https://fred.stlouisfed.org/series/UMCSENT

Tesla. (2024, January 24). *Tesla Investor Relations*. Ir.tesla.com. https://ir.tesla.com/#quarterly-disclosure

SEC.gov | EDGAR - Search and Access. (n.d.). www.sec.gov.
https://www.sec.gov/edgar/search-and-access

Tesla, Inc. (TSLA) Stock Price, News, Quote & History - Yahoo Finance. (n.d.). Ca.finance.yahoo.com.
https://ca.finance.yahoo.com/quote/TSLA/